D0513123

THE FEMINIST LIBRARY
AND INFORMATION CENTRE
5–5a Westminster Bridge Road
London S.E.1
Telephone: 01–928 7789

A SUPPRESSED CRY

Life and Death of a
Quaker Daughter

Victoria
Glendinning

New Introduction by the Author

THE FEMINIST LIBRARY
AND INFORMATION CENTRE
5–5a Westminster Bridge Road
London S.E.1
Telephone: 01-928 7789

Published by VIRAGO PRESS Limited 1995
20 Vauxhall Bridge Road, London SW1V 2SA

First published by Routledge & Kegan Paul Ltd, London 1969

A CIP catalogue record for this book is available from the British Library.

Typeset by Keystroke, Jacaranda Lodge, Wolverhampton
Printed and bound in Great Britain by
Cox & Wyman Ltd, Reading, Berkshire

For my father
Frederic Seebohm

Contents

Acknowledgements

I should like to thank my father and my Seebohm uncles and aunts for letting me use the material which made this book.

I should also like to thank the following :
Mrs Mabel Elizabeth Christie; The Principal and Fellows of Newnham College, Cambridge; The City Librarian, Bradford; Dr Greta Hottinger; The Public Record Office; Mrs Humphrey Madden; The Director, Metropolitan Police Forensic Science Laboratory; The Principal of Bedford College, London (for the use of Dame Margaret Tuke's unpublished Autobiographical Notes).

For the growing good of the world is partly dependent on un-historic acts; and that things are not so ill with you and me as they might have been, is half owing to the number who lived faithfully a hidden life, and rest in unvisited tombs.

George Eliot

No one will be much or little, except in some one else's mind – so be careful of the minds you get into.

Djuna Barnes

New Introduction

In the dining-room of my parents' house near Ware in Hertfordshire there stood a tall cabinet. Its lower drawers were stuffed with family letters and papers. My father would urge me to take a look at them. The material about his Aunt Winnie, he said, was very touching. She had been one of the early students at Newnham College, Cambridge, and died of asthma in 1885 at the age of 22. He had inherited the cabinet, and its contents, on the death of Winnie's last surviving sister Esther in 1951.

My father and his brothers and sister constituted the third generation of Seebohms to be based in Hertfordshire. My brother, my sister and I were sometimes taken to tea with our Great-Aunt Esther in Hitchin as children. She lived in the house to which Winnie had been taken when she was dying – but I had never heard of Winnie, in those days. I barely recall Great-Aunt Esther, but I remember a dark dining-room with a white cloth on the table, an elaborately set tea, and the necessity to behave well.

So I resisted my father, refusing to take an interest in his family history.

Then, during a week in May 1966, staying at my parents' with my first husband and our children – we had four under seven at the time – I succumbed. I began reading the letters and papers, and took them home with me. But it was another year before I began working properly on what was to become this book. I don't think I aspired, then, to be a professional writer, though I wanted to do *something*. I applied to Southampton

University to do a one-year post-graduate diploma course in Social Administration, a basic social-work qualification.

Winnie's story, when I finished writing it, became *A Suppressed Cry* – or rather, it became the brown-paper package that I sent off on its travels again as soon as it flopped back through our letter-box, as it repeatedly did. I knew no authors apart from academics, I knew no publishers, agents or editors. I copied the names and addresses of publishing firms from the books on our shelves, choosing a new one, at random, each time the typescript was returned with a rejection slip. When I received a letter signed 'Colin Franklin' from Routledge & Kegan Paul – the seventh or eighth publisher that I had tried – saying that he would be pleased to publish it, I was astonished. I had already begun the diploma course.

I went up to London from Southampton to meet Colin Franklin on a Tuesday afternoon in October 1968. Routledge was then in Carter Lane in the City. It was just as I always imagined a publisher's office to be (and no longer ever is). I went up dusty stairs with books piled on the treads to Colin's room, which was more like a don's study than an office.

The book's publication in November 1969 coincided with the beginning of my first social-work job, and we were already preoccupied with the possibility of moving to Dublin. I was thrilled when the finished copies of *A Suppressed Cry* arrived, but there was no reason to go to London for the publication. The book appeared without me, as it were. It received some nice reviews. Since then it has slept undisturbed.

The *New Statesman*, in October 1969, said that 'Mrs Glendinning writes so well and so succinctly that she should be encouraged to spread herself in further books'. Colin Franklin was among those who encouraged me, but though he remains a great friend, he never published another book of mine. There wasn't one to publish for another eight years, by which time he had moved on. During those years, writing was not my main preoccupation, though I began reviewing, and made false starts with a biography and a novel. Not until *Elizabeth Bowen* (1977) was I back on course.

I have, as the *New Statesman* advised, learnt to spread myself a bit. I did minimal research for *A Suppressed Cry* – partly because I had little free time and little opportunity to be away from home – but chiefly because I didn't really know how to go about it. These factors, plus a temperamental fear of boring people, which I retain, account for this book's shortness and its succinct quality. I did visit Newnham, and Hitchin Museum, and I read Hitchin newspapers of the period in the newspaper library at Colindale. I questioned older relations and sought out the descendants of Winnie's friends; and I consulted the Metropolitan Police Forensic Science lab, to see whether they had the technology to decipher what had been written on the deliberately torn-away portion of a crucial letter, from the marks left on the page beneath. (No luck.) I absorbed the historical background from books of social history and memoirs, and in the small back bedroom of our house in Southampton I worked on the Seebohm letters and diaries.

Reading the book now, I am quite surprised by the confident feminism of its approach. I did not know that I had reached that point so soon. The first Virago books were still five years away in the future. The only modern feminist book that had come my way before I wrote *A Suppressed Cry* was Betty Friedan's *The Feminine Mystique*, which made a huge impression on me. Later, a dashing academic colleague of my husband's, Jean Franco, stayed a night with us. I remember her watching me thoughtfully, in silence, while I did the ironing. I still do the ironing, there's nothing wrong with that. But as a thank-you for the visit, Jean sent me Eva Figes's *Patriarchal Attitudes*, which became my second landmark-book.

Though *A Suppressed Cry* was published by the time I read Eva Figes's book, 'patriarchal attitudes' are at the heart of the matter. There are two casualties in the close, loving family I describe in this story – Winnie herself, and her sister Freda. I wish I had found out more about the nature of Freda's mental breakdowns, and about the kind of treatment she received. So far as Winnie is concerned, I wish I had read rather more about asthmatic illness, and thought rather more about her difficulty in swallowing. After the book was published, a friend who was a medical student suggested that Winnie might have been anorexic. It may seem extraordinary, but in 1969 there was absolutely no public awareness of anorexia, and the phrase 'eating disorder' would have suggested to me only the anarchy of a family meal in our kitchen.

There is another way in which the allegedly swinging 60s seem nearly as close in spirit to Winnie's day as to our own. Leafing just now through the letters from strangers who had liked *A Suppressed Cry*, I found two, from men, addressed formally to my then husband, asking him to pass on to me their appreciation of the book. Presumably they thought that he would not approve of my receiving letters from strange gentlemen. This notion of what was proper is like a residual echo from the world that Trollope knew.

I would be better equipped to write about Winnie now than I was then. After my parents died in 1990, more photographs and family memorabilia came to light. My brother Richard Seebohm did a lot of research on our Seebohm antecedents for a paper he read to the Hitchin

Historical Society in 1994. Until I read my brother's paper, I had not known that Winnie's Uncle Benjamin Seebohm lived nearby and was prominent in the Luton branch of the bank, Sharples & Co – properly Sharples, Tuke, Lucas & Seebohm. Winnie's sister Juliet, when referring cryptically to Winnie's disallowed love affair, mentioned their Aunt Julia as a parallel case. I wish I had investigated the story of this Julia Seebohm, who married Joseph Rowntree of the York chocolate firm, and died soon after. Nor was I properly familiar with all the intricate connections that link the Seebohms with other Quaker clans in a tight genealogical spiral. I had not realised that the family remained sufficiently close to their German roots for my father Frederic, Winnie's nephew, to be called 'Fritzi', a nickname that was strategically abandoned at the onset of the First World War, when he was five*.

Indeed I hardly knew Hitchin itself in the late 1960s, though in my early childhood I had often stayed in the nearby village of Preston, at the house called Poynder's End built for my grandfather – Winnie's adored brother Hugh – at the turn of the century. Then, eight years after A *Suppressed Cry* was published, my second husband Terence de Vere White and I bought a cottage in another village near Hitchin, where we remained for ten years.

It was during those years that I grew to know the distinctive 'look' of the Hertfordshire landscape that Winnie's sister Juliet painted in watercolours. (Esther painted too, but Juliet did much more. Everyone in the family has 'Aunt Juliets' hanging on their walls. While we lived in Hertfordshire, yet another cache of them was found in Hitchin, in a music school – Esther's former home, where I had been to tea as a child.) I learned the Seebohms' home town properly, and walked regularly

*At the same time and for the same reason, my mother's Jewish father, whose family had, like the Seebohms, first settled in Bradford, was changing the family name from Herz to Hurst.

down the wide street called Bancroft where they lived. Towards the end of our time there, I wrote a book about Hertfordshire, discovering in the process a great deal about the Hitchin of Winnie's day which could have made A *Suppressed Cry* a more solid contribution to local history.

In short I could, had I waited, have written a longer and a different book. It might not have been a more telling one. Too much information can blur the issues.

My recent attachment to Hitchin and Hertfordshire, and some of what I now knew about life and work there in the 1880s, went into the novel *Electricity* (1995). The fictional Charlotte, transplanted to a house near Hitchin from a grubby London suburb, must have coincided many times with the real-life Winnie, shopping in the market-place. The dates fit exactly. Yet this never once occurred to me while I was writing the novel. Until, after *Electricity* was published, I re-read A *Suppressed Cry* for the purposes of this edition, I had no idea that there were other startling (to me) points of contact between the two young women. Charlotte did everything Winnie did not, and vice versa, but neither escaped their fate. They are mirror images of the same predicament.

I had quite forgotten about Winnie, even though her portrait by Juliet – the one reproduced on the cover of this book – hangs in my bedroom. She was there, in another sense, all the time. She still is. 'But they are all dead now', I wrote, when I came to the end of the story. That's not quite right. In some loop of space-time they are always there in the sunlit Hermitage garden in Hitchin; just as I am still in the back bedroom in Southampton putting together my first book. In any case, family stories have no endings.

Victoria Glendinning, London 1995

1

Frederic and Mary Ann

Everything has changed, and nothing has changed.

This is the true story of a young woman who lived in the later part of Queen Victoria's reign. But do not be misled into thinking that because it is history it has nothing to do with you. 1885 is yesterday. It is probably tomorrow too.

The dramatis personae are Mr and Mrs Frederic Seebohm of Hitchin and their six children – Juliet, Esther, Winnie, Freda, Hugh and Hilda. The heroine is the third daughter, Winnie.

Frederic Seebohm is a Quaker, second son of the evangelical Quaker Benjamin Seebohm who had come to England from Germany in 1814 and settled in Bradford. Benjamin married Esther Wheeler of Hitchin and they had four children: Henry, who became a distinguished ornithologist; Frederic; Julia, who died in childbirth on the first anniversary of her marriage; and another Benjamin.

Frederic's remarkable father and his Yorkshire childhood endowed him with a strong family feeling, a firm allegiance to the Society of Friends, and an education at Bootham, the Friends' school in York. But there was no money.

It was decided that he should read for the Bar, and he entered the London chambers of J. Bevan Braithwaite. It was at this time that he first came to live in Hitchin. An early commuter, he found it cheaper to live in lodgings in Hitchin and travel up by the day, and easier to concentrate on his books in the evenings without the noise and distractions of London life. Hitchin was very much a backwater in those days. As late as 1885, an official report on its statistics remarks that it was 'not one of those places which advance rapidly in population'. In spite of the railway, in the ten years 1871–1881 its population actually decreased.

In such a small community Frederic soon found friends and connections among the Hitchin Quakers. There have been Quakers in Hitchin since the 1650s, and in the nineteenth century there was an influential clan of them – Tukes, Lucases, Ransoms, Extons, Wheelers – most of them middle-class and prosperous, though cut off from the 'county' by reason of their noncomformity, and from other noncomformists by their exclusiveness and wealth, nonconformism being largely a lower-class phenomenon.

Young Frederic in the 1850s became especially friendly with the William Extons, and fell in love with their younger daughter, Mary Ann. She was reputedly beautiful – she was known as the 'Jewel of Hitchin'. She was indubitably rich – her father was a partner in the thriving Hitchin bank of Sharples and Co. On their engagement in 1856, Frederic describes her as 'the gentle, loving and confiding sharer of both joys and sorrows' and as 'a jewel concealed under a gentle and unpretending exterior.'

Be that as it may, the wealth and local standing of his bride's family determined the way Frederic's life was to develop. For one thing, the Extons were unwilling to let their Jewel be dragged away to darkest Bradford, where Frederic had been intending to return. For another thing, the ease of life which money brings with it made it possible for him to pursue the academic interests for which he was to be chiefly remembered.

So he married Mary Ann and became a junior partner in her father's bank. And when Mary Ann's parents died, they inherited the Hermitage – a large house, or rather an agglomeration of houses of different periods, in the street called Bancroft in Hitchin. The Hermitage had forty rooms, seven acres of garden, and was maintained by a living-in staff of five or six servants, three gardeners, a groom and a stable-boy.

Mary Ann's widowed mother died in 1860, leaving a rather spectacular will. She seems not to have been too happy about

Frederic's capability of keeping her daughter in the style to which she was accustomed. Mary Ann had already brought Frederic ten thousand pounds as a marriage portion. According to her mother's will she was now left valuable stocks and shares, the income from which was to be for her own separate use, 'free from the control of the said Frederic Seebohm', and not to be used for the payment of any debts that he might incur.

Nor was this all. By arrangement with the other Jewel, her elder daughter Margaret who was already married to the rich Norfolk banker Joseph Gurney Barclay, Mrs Exton bequeathed to Mary Ann

> all my wearing apparel, watches, trinkets, jewels and other personal ornaments, and also my household goods, and furniture, plate, plated articles, china, glass, linen, books, maps, prints, pictures, musical intruments, wines, liquors, stock of fuel and all the other household property and effects whatsoever.

Also five thousand pounds for immediate expenses. Also, of course, the Hermitage itself. Mary Ann was a Jewel indeed.

Here Frederic remained until the end of his life. He also remained a junior partner of Sharples and Co. But he developed his talents in other fields to the point where H. A. L. Fisher could describe him after his death as 'a brilliant Englishman who was held in deep affection and regard by a wide circle of friends'. And wide it was; he counted among his friends distinguished scholars such as Max Müller and Sir Paul Vinogradoff, and was acquainted with many of the leading academics and politicians of his day.

His academic reputation was largely based on his researches into early systems of land-tenure, published in 1883 as *The English Village Community*, which traced the early Saxon system of tenure back to the Roman occupation. Contemporary historians did not all like the idea that English freedom was rooted in Roman slavery, and Frederic's theories never won universal acceptance. But the three fields of Hitchin manor became the classic instance appealed to on questions of land tenure. Frederic Seebohm and his theories were taken seriously.

His other publications also received – and receive – respectful notice, notably works on Sir Thomas More and Erasmus, and a much-used text-book, *The Era of the Protestant Revolution*.

These achievements made him well-known in academic circles, and gained him by the end of his life honorary degrees from Oxford, Cambridge and Edinburgh. It is remarkable how someone with no academic background, a banker in a country town, could become a recognised authority and a historian among historians. In the same way, James Hack Tuke, senior partner in the same Hitchin bank, became an authority on the Irish problem and was consulted and used by the Government.

In Frederic's case the lack of academic training showed, as it must.

Vinogradoff in his obituary of Frederic said that he had the merits and the defects of the self-taught man; he did not pay much attention to what had been done or what was being done by others. Vinogradoff compared him to 'a brilliant chess-player, always intent upon the attack, but sometimes failing to guard his positions against the adversary'.

This was Frederic as seen by eminent outsiders. For Hitchin, as the century advanced, he was the well-known banker and Friend, deeply involved in local politics and local philanthropic projects. For Winnie and her brother and sisters he was the adored paterfamilias, who knew everything and whose word was law. And the dominant figure of Papa shaped their lives and personalities, both for good and for ill.

*

It was not after all so very long ago. But there is an envelope, addressed to Miss Juliet Seebohm and postmarked 1883, which has a scribbled pencil message across the back: 'George Gillett is ill in Typhoid Fever and his little girl has died in it. Bevan Braithwaite's cook is also ill in the same fever'.

This is the big difference between them and us. People died all the time, young people and children, from illnesses which are now curable or hardly exist. Consumption was still widespread; as Black's Medical Dictionary then put it, 'symptoms of consumption are well known, since there are few who have not had an opportunity of observing the disease in some relative or friend'. Any young girl with a cough that did not seem to get better was watched with morbid anxiety by her near and dear. If you were poor, you died of consumption fairly quickly. If you were rich, you were taken to Switzerland or the South of France, where the big hotels were quite used to receiving invalids and their keepers. The keepers would form lasting friendships with one another as they pushed bath-chairs and observed symptoms. But the patients died in the end, whether in the slums of Birmingham or in Nice. Meta Tuke, Winnie's best friend, lost two sisters this way.

The causes of many diseases were still not known and in many cases not even looked for, while fainting-fits were well-known to be catching. Meta Tuke was tripped up when playing tennis one day, and fell unconscious:

> I awoke to find myself on a sofa surrounded by a number of anxious faces. In answer to my desire at once to return to the game, I was urged to remain quiet until a doctor arrived. As I consented there was a crash. My partner, the cause of my disaster, fell in a dead faint. While he was being restored, another fall. Beatrice Horner (she and my partner, Mr Richardson, were subsequently married) also succumbed to a faint, and a little later the children's nursery governess followed her example. The party was spoiled, the hostess rather shattered.

The importance of hygiene and proper sanitation was only just beginning to be understood, and only the most progressive of young women knew anything about it; such as the Squire's unpopular daughter in Tennyson's dialect ballad *The Village Wife* who outraged a bereaved mother:

> An I thowt 'twur the will o' the Lord,
> But Miss Annie she said it wur draäins.

A lot of chronic stomach trouble, including the 'bilious attacks' which James Hack Tuke suffered all his life, can be attributed to drains. Plumbing installed with tremendous pride around the middle of the century makes modern hair stand on end; the soil pipe generally joined the bath outlet pipe with no trap, so that all manner of effluvia escaped in all directions. Terrible smells penetrated even into the most ceremonious drawing rooms.

Women enjoyed ill-health more frequently than men. This was partly due to the hazards of too-frequent confinements, which left many women permanently on sofas as unspecified invalids, and partly to boredom. For it was boring to be a woman in the nineteenth century. It was boring, that is, to be a lady.

That is so easily said. It is a cliché. What is more difficult is to feel what it really means. Every normal person lives through pockets of tedium and time-filling. It was as if these were all that there was to life, infinitely extended and morally enforced. A lady was not supposed to have any desires or functions outside her home duties. Her only way out was to get married – and that changed nothing except her status and her surroundings. Her life was still circumscribed by rules, conventions and rituals.

Even personal relations, her only contact with a wider world, were ritualised. *Manners and Rules of Good Society* by a Member of the Aristocracy, published in the eighteen-nineties, suggests that a lady having a large acquaintance

> should keep a visiting book in which to enter the names of her acquaintances, and the date when their cards were left upon her, and the date of her return cards left upon them, that she might know whether a card were due to her from them, or whether it were due from them to her. A lady having a small acquaintance would find a memorandum book sufficient for the purpose.

Clearly this could fill up a morning nicely. And the implication seems to be that if you find a memorandum book sufficient you should be worried.

Girls of high intelligence and an enquiring mind were the ones who suffered most. They seem like lonely bonfires, burning away their frustration and emptiness into their diaries and private letters. Florence Nightingale in 1852, before her working life had begun, wrote:

> Passion, intellect, moral activity – these three have never been satisfied in a woman. In this cold and oppressive conventional atmosphere, they cannot be satisfied.

Women, she complained, were expected to be available at any hour of the day for any trivial purpose. Was this because man's time was more valuable than woman's, she asked? Or simply because woman had confessedly nothing to do? The only accepted reasons for a woman having an 'occupation' were widowhood or want of bread. Otherwise she filled her time with domestic duties, which were for the most part, the acid Florence said, bad habits. Anyhow all the real work was done by servants. 'This system dooms some minds to incurable infancy, others to silent misery.'

Anne Clough, another bonfire, was a youngish spinster with no prospects in the north of England, and she kept a diary.

> 'I sometimes think,' she wrote in 1841, 'that there is no use bothering myself so about learning things. I certainly don't know why I do try to learn so many things, but I feel a great impulse to do it, therefore I think I must . . . I sometimes fancy I shall do great things, but will it not all come to nothing? Yet I should like never to be forgotten, to do something great for my country which would make my name live for ever. But I am only a woman.'

Anne Clough became the first Principal of Newnham College, Cambridge, and was still in office when Winnie Seebohm and Meta Tuke went up in 1885. She, and Florence Nightingale, Emily Davis, George Eliot, Elizabeth Garrett Anderson, Beatrice Webb and all the other famous names, they broke through. But what of all the other thousands of girls, with perhaps no less talent, who never made it? Poor doused bonfires, who poured out their frustrations in long-lost diaries, whom no one has ever heard of, nor ever will. They became the sad creatures described by Anne Clough later to her students as 'restless and unhappy, struggling for they knew not what. Many suffered grievously, some fell into ill-health, many were soured and spent their lives in foolish and useless complaining'.

As time passes the bonfires blaze more openly as each one comes to realise that she is not alone. Meanwhile we must see our female characters against a background of futility and fussiness, however comfortable and idyllic the foreground may appear. For lack of outside commitments, they used their energies worrying about their health, both spiritual and physical. Winnie's mama, the cossetted Jewel of Hitchin, larded her love-letters to her fiancé with bulletins about her tiredness, her bad throat and her face-ache. Even George Eliot, an intellectual who knew better than anyone what society did to women, was infected. Winnie in 1885 was reading her published letters and was 'much struck by the fact that *clever women* seem to write of nothing but the state of their health and the temperature at which their spirits stand!'

In Winnie's life-time as now there was the usual uncomfortable co-existence of prejudice and enlightenment. Religion would never be quite so easy after Darwin. Karl Marx was already in his grave in Highgate cemetery by 1883, when *The Bitter Cry of Outcast London*, produced by nonconformist ministers, exposed the appalling living conditions of the London poor. This report and others like it led to a Royal Commission on the Housing of the Working Classes. And yet Octavia Hill, an acknowledged authority on the subject, was excluded from the Commission because she was a woman. What was much worse, a certain J. Baldwin Brown could write in 1880:

> The poor have the Gospel preached to them still, and many a cup of pure bright pleasure does it lift to their lips . . . . they went back to their poor hovels, their cabbage, their crust, and their dull monotonous task, feeling that life was not all a bare dry desert.

Some people were still incapable of the lateral thinking which would suggest that it would be more worthwhile to improve on the poor hovels, the cabbage and the crust, rather than to resign people to putting up with them.

Even in Hitchin, the little kingdom of the truly philanthropic and thoughtful Tukes and Seebohms, one must not expect too much. Everything was done to alleviate the wretchedness of the lower classes, but nobody was thinking in terms of classlessness. The barriers remained erect even for the annual Flower Show held in Frederic's meadow. There were separate competitions for 'Ladies' and for 'Women'. The ladies competed with elegant floral arrangements. In July 1885 Miss Winnie Seebohm won a Third Prize for 'a terra cotta jar filled with very luxuriant honeysuckle'. In the class called 'Harmony in Purple and Grey', First, Second and Third Prizes were won by the Misses Juliet, Hilda and Esther Seebohm. Other Ladies' Prizes were carried off by the various Misses Ransom, Tuke and Lucas.

The Women, however, were not expected to be interested in flowers, even though it was a Flower Show. Their competitions were for laundry-work, ironing, preserving, and sewing plain shirts. And the winners in each class are referred to as, to take an example, Emily Bottoms, with no nonsense about Miss.

I suppose there was never any doubt about which category one belonged to.

Winnie was lucky to be born into a Quaker family. Things had changed for the Quakers since the beginning of the century. In those days there had been a distinction between Strict Quakers and those who were not so strict. A Strict Quaker such as Elizabeth Fry the prison reformer dressed in the plain Quaker habit at all times, even on full-dress occasions. Music and dancing were out. Even painting was dangerous, on account of the unbridling effect of colours. If the son of a Strict Quaker married outside the Society of Friends his family could not attend the wedding, and the errant child was cast out of the Society. Thus families became increasingly inbred, with predictable results. It was certainly hard to be a Strict Quaker, and young people especially suffered greatly surpressing their guilty longings for what were, for most people, perfectly normal amusements. 'The World has dried up since those days' wrote one of Elizabeth Fry's daughters in 1870. But not many Quaker sons and daughters would agree with her. Generations of social isolation meant that the clan feeling was still very strong; and what remained of the Quaker tradition by the last quarter of the century was the best part.

On the highest level of English intellectual and political life, certain families emerged in the nineteenth-century to form a powerful clique, united by blood, interest and tradition. These were the Huxleys, Macaulays, Arnolds, Darwins, Wedgwoods, Trevelyans and their many connections and satellites. The English Quakers formed a comparable but far less influential solar system. They were mostly prosperous bankers and merchants, with enclaves in all the principal cities and particular strongholds in Norfolk, Hertfordshire, Yorkshire and the West Country. The names are many but they recur: Barclay, Hoare, Buxton, Seebohm, Tuke, Ransom, Lucas, Wheeler, Gillett, Rowntree, Exton, Leatham, Fry, Clark. They still intermarried, and visited each other constantly. These family visits, often lasting several weeks, are a feature of most Victorian middle-class lives. In fact Caroline Jebb, an American bride in Cambridge in the 1870's, said:

English people are very fond of jaunting about to see their friends and relations; they seem to me the most restless of nations!

The point was, or so it seems now, that it gave the women and girls something to do. The preparation for an expected visit, the complicated travelling arrangements, the organised entertainment for one's own guests and for the guests of one's friends, filled the spaces that were their days. It must have been great fun – but it assumed an importance that only an idle society could tolerate.

A good tradition that the Quakers preserved into Winnie's time, and in which they still continue, was the sense of duty and social responsibility which implies that one is on earth to improve the lot of others. This inclination actually became more marked as Quakers became less isolated and allowed themselves to become involved, both locally and nationally, in politics, education and administration.

In addition, Quakers had always had the reputation of educat-cating their children well – including their daughters. And this last was perhaps what Winnie and her sisters had most to be grateful for.

2

The Family

One day in the 1870's, Mary Ann Seebohm took a little note-book about two inches by four and wrote in it her memories of her children as babies. 'Children' she began in her tiny copper-plate handwriting 'are the delight of one's life.'

The first delight, born in 1859, was a daughter, Juliet Mary. She was intelligent, and 'when scarcely more than a year old would point to some letters of the Alphabet when asked them'. Frederic and Mary Ann believed in discipline. When Juliet was about two years old she started to come downstairs for Reading – the Quaker equivalent of family prayers – and would some-times, not suprisingly, be very restless; 'but after having to sit still awhile on the sofa after it was finished, she soon overcame this habit, and has never been any trouble since, either there or in Meeting, to which she began to go when four years old'.

Two years later another daughter was born named Esther Margaret, generally called Essie. Poor Essie as a child is re-corded as being very shy, 'which helped to form passionate out-breaks, which were often very trying'. But she must have worked it all out in childhood. Later in life she was reticent but serene, with a nice sense of humour which some of the others lacked.

The third daughter was Winnie, officially Wilhelmina, born on April 10th 1863. Her two elder sisters were plain little girls. Mary Ann writes: 'Our Baby was a plumper and prettier child than the other two had been, so that she was styled our little Moon-Faced Chick.' Her hair was golden-red, so that she was nicknamed by her sisters 'Lion' or 'Lonnie'. She must have been an uncomplicated baby, for her mother goes straight on to deplore Essie's 'wild-goat antics', and to describe yet another sister who was born two years later. Mary Ann produced her babies every other April, regular as clockwork; it would be unwise to draw any conclusions from this observation.

This fourth daughter was Freda, rather an anxiety right from the beginning. 'A frail child was this little darling. A very tender baby she was, and she has continued a sensitive little thing, both in body and mind – a most loving child and very companionable for her age tho' not so forward as the others in learning.'

With their fifth child the Seebohms achieved a son and heir:

A little *boy* was born on April 4th 1867 – and a very precious gift was he felt to be to us. He has been a bright little boy showing signs of early intelligence – was very fond of pictures and remembered the names of animals and birds very readily when a year to eighteen months old. Though a healthy baby he has been liable to bronchial attacks which have at times caused us great anxiety. Though quite a boy by nature he is very gentle and loving, and very sensitive to reproof.

The bright little boy was named Hugh Exton, and his favourite companion and confidante thoughout childhood and after was Freda, the sister nearest him in age.

'The last of the little flock', Hilda, was born in 1870. 'A darling pet is she, but not so much of a cosset being of a much more independent nature and apparently of more robust health.'

After producing her little flock, the Jewel of Hitchin begins to fade. In this united family the little girls when away from home wrote to their sisters more often than to their mother. Mary Ann is usually on the sofa, or, on their holiday excursions, being pushed in a bath chair. She was probably the victim of some undiagnosed female complaint. Of course they loved her, especially as little children, and especially Freda: 'Gentle loving Freda said to me one day, I do love you so Mama, I love you with all my heart!' She was a good woman; when she died an old friend said that in the thirty years she had known her, she had never heard Mary Ann speak an unkind word about a neighbour. But it is hardly surprising that in this overwhelmingly feminine household, all the sisters' pride and admiration should be lavished on clever little brother Hugh and on marvellous Papa who knew everything. Mother's influence gradually became restricted to the sphere of watching over her children's health, reminding them to wear their overcoats, and observing their comings and goings through an open door. 'Mother is still upstairs,' wrote Hugh to an absent sister, 'which she makes an opportunity for seeing who is going where, and with what jacket.'

It was a happy childhood. It could hardly fail to be. Hitchin was an idyllic setting for an idyllic family life. It remained until the end of the century a small country town. It was, with Mitcham, the chief lavender-growing area of England, and Hitchin noses were assailed in turn by the sweet smell of the lavender-fields and the paradoxically nasty smell of the lavender processing works. The women and girls in the poor houses at the foot of Windmill Hill sat in their doorways plaiting straw for the straw-hat industry.

The Hermitage itself was a paradise for children. The garden and grounds extended in all directions, with access to outlying parts facilitated by two tunnels under local roads. Through one of the tunnels, the Hitchin river flowed parallel to the path. There were lawns, flowers, vegetables, woods and water. The house itself was a jumble of different periods; the Tudor part was renovated to the tune of a thousand pounds when the children were growing up, making a smoking-room for Hugh and a billiard room, beautifully panelled in elm by Barker the local carpenter, and preserving the old priest-hole with its air-tube into the hall. But the core of the house was the central section, where the library and the drawing-room opened on to the terrace and lawn. The library was where Frederic worked at his books, and through it there was a further little room where he kept his first editions and Erasmus collection. Above this sanctum was the girls' private sitting-room. Down in the drawing-room Mother sat on the sofa reading and writing letters, with the great chiffonier behind her and her eyes on the two pairs of high double doors. It was a haphazard sort of house; the girls' bedrooms led off each other, up or down one or two steps; for some reason or other the great mahogany bath was built into a corner of Freda's bedroom. Heaven knows up what attic stairs slept Eliza the cook, Shekel the head housemaid, and all the others. Giddings the coachman had a cottage across the street.

The family had everything in their favour: material comfort, a large and loving family, and a close circle of friends. The family they saw most of was the Tukes, whose house was nearly opposite the Hermitage. Meta, the Tukes' youngest child, was Winnie's special friend. 'It was not an emotional friendship,' said Meta, 'but an alliance of two natures of different tempers which fitted each other'.

Meta was tiny with huge eyes. She described herself as 'very small and easily embraced'. But she had an independent and sceptical mind. During an extended phase of religious fervour, Juliet, Esther and Winnie used to hold bible meetings in the summerhouse at the bottom of the Tukes' garden, the object of which was to increase their capacity for faith in order to be able to move mountains. Meta attended the meetings and was affected by the atmosphere, 'but it was in a cold, unreceptive spirit'. Much later, when she took with difficulty the great step of going up to Newnham, she insisted that she was only going as an Enquirer.

Winnie was quite different. She was impulsive and ardent and desperately involved in whatever she did. This is how Meta described her:

Fair in form, figure and colouring; a mind quick to learn and retain its learning; sensitive to all artistic appeal and the master of all she undertook, she shone still more in her singular integrity of character and in her utter unawareness of her prowess. In all we did together she excelled me; music and painting, flowers, dancing and acting – games of all sorts (she was the best tennis player in our circle) – in all our studies she was *facile princeps* yet never put me to shame.

But that was written much later. Meanwhile the little Seebohms and Tukes played away their days. They went away on visits to relatives in batches, and missed each other when parted. Winnie, thirteen years old, writes to Juliet and Esther:

> Home is *so* dull without you two little dears, it really is enough to try the patience of an oyster. Hilda sends her bestest love to you and is going to draw you some kisses. It is so dull without my two dear sisters, I am pining for you! *Do* write to me soon and write a very long letter too! Of course I have nothing to tell you as you only went today, it seems as if you had been away for years.

They occupied themselves with their pets. The Tuke girls kept chickens and the Seebohms kept cats and kittens. As Winnie said, cats seemed to be the only animals that did well at the Hermitage. Esther's diary for 1880 begins with the mournful entry 'Jack drowned in pond'. Jack was a dog and the experiment was not repeated for years.

What else did they do? They made birthday cards and Christmas cards for relations, friends and servants. They made Valentines for everybody, regardless of age or sex. They trimmed hats for poor children, made scrapbooks to send to the Infirmary, dressed dolls for bazaars, wrote and delivered lectures to each other on the books they were reading. They played badminton, learnt songs, produced plays, practised the piano, painted in water-colours, pressed flowers, and tormented their Mademoiselle 'who has such queer ideas and is *so* absurd sometimes that we can't help exploding which makes her somewhat ferocious, it is very naughty of us but you can't imagine how absurd she is!'

And when they were poorly, which was quite often, they were given paregoric, sweet nitre, blackcurrant tea, linseed tea, mustard poultices, and an infinity of gargles.

The two families were more or less parallel in early days. Both fathers went off every morning to the Bank, where James Hack Tuke was senior partner. Both families consisted of a cluster of daughters and one son – though Sam Tuke was a good deal older than Hugh. With the education of their sons, Frederic Seebohm and James Tuke continued the move away from traditional Quaker isolation. They made their sons into regular

English gentlemen. Hugh was sent to Rugby, a school which was based on the Anglican faith and the monitorial system. A school such as Rugby was not as exclusive as Eton, Winchester or Harrow, and the boys from professional or business backgrounds who went there emerged to swell the ranks of the enlarging upper middle class. Both Hugh and Sam went on to Cambridge, which was still a new departure for Quakers, though noncomformists had been accepted since 1856.

The conflict between school and college life and his family background had a disturbing effect on Sam Tuke. It was, after all, lonely to be a Friend. It was still something to live down. At Cambridge Sam threw off his Quaker restraints – he danced, played cards and went to theatres. 'Not that these things were done in excess,' wrote his little sister Meta, 'but they filled his life'. When he came home he quarrelled with his father, who was easy to quarrel with, and criticised his sisters for their lack of the social graces. His mother and his eldest sister had recently died of consumption. 'Life was not easy at home' said Meta. Things were better for the Seebohms in the Hermitage over the road. Hugh did not react so violently to his exposure to Rugby and the wider world. Maybe it would have been easier for him in the long run if he had.

Meanwhile the children were growing up. And that is where for so many young people like them, particularly the girls, life began to seem just a little less sweet. For a routine that is totally fulfilling for a child – a round of pets and walks and aunts and bazaars and regular meals – is not a rich enough prospect for an intelligent energetic young woman. ('I hate Bazaars! and Fancy Work too!' said Winnie). And yet that is just what the future held for most girls; more of the same, for ever. If your father had enough money to keep you, marriage was the only possible reason for leaving home.

Meta's elder sister Minnie did marry in 1877 at the age of eighteen. It does not sound a very romantic match. Edward Lindsell was a solicitor and rose-fancier, rather set in his ways, eleven years older than she, and he wanted a wife. After the wedding Frances Tuke said to Meta, '*We* will not be silly about young men, will we?' And they never were.

Not that they had much opportunity. The Seebohm and Tuke families, with their single sons and many daughters, were typical. As Meta said:

The shortage of young men was a very notable feature of our girlhood. In the large families in our neighbourhood, there would be perhaps one, at most two, boys, with from five to nine girls. It can be well understood that this inequality of the sexes, together with the carefully chaperoned existence of the girls, led to a rather unnatural society. Too high an importance (in their own eyes and that of others) came to be attached to the few – too much shyness and repression on the part of the many. Only the bolder girls could count on a high time.

You may safely suppose that Juliet, Esther, Winnie, Freda and Hilda did not have a high time, at least not in the sense that Meta meant. No Quaker girl would have been among the bolder ones. And only Winnie had looks.

But being Quakers had its compensations. For the girls, un- like most of their 'county' neighbours, were being properly educated. They had a French Mademoiselle and a German Fraülein. The Fraülein seems to have been of higher calibre than the absurd Mademoiselle, but not so high-powered as her remarkable pupils:

'She informed me,' wrote Winnie, 'I suppose in reply to a too ambitious request on my part, that Klopstock's *Messias* was too sublime for *anybody* to read all through in a lifetime. It puzzled my young mind sorely that one man should be able to write what no other man was capable of reading! Looking back now, hers seems to me such a remarkable mind that should I ever write a novel I shall certainly put her into it. She prided herself on being a freethinker and upon tolerating atheistical friends, and yet no-one was ever so incapable of receiving a new thought or revising a judgement once passed. This led to many a discussion which may have served to stimulate German conversation but never had any practical result. I remember a hot debate which lasted for many days, in which I upheld the superiority of the Athenians and she preferred the Spartans. Another standing quarrel was Carlyle, until one day it came out that she had never read anything except an extract in a literature book from the *French Revolution!*'

The girls studied Latin, French, German, Mathematics, History, Botany, English Literature, and the rudiments of Greek and Italian at home. Botany and Natural History were strong family interests. Uncle Henry, Frederic's elder brother, was a distinguished naturalist and published several standard works on birds, besides running a lucrative steel manufactory in Sheffield.

Juliet and Esther and later Hilda even went away to school in London, to Bedford College. It was not in the 1870's the distinguished academic establishment it is today. It had been founded in 1860 by a Mrs Reid for the serious education of school-age girls, without any aggressively feminist image. In Mrs Reid's own words:

My dearest wish is that the whole proceeding may be as an Underground Railway, differing in this from the American U.R. that no-one shall ever know of its existence. You will thus be saved all importunity and much vexation of various kinds.

It should perhaps be explained that by 'Underground Railway' Mrs Reid was not referring to an early version of the Tube but to the secret channels through which the Abolitionists assisted fugitive slaves to escape to Canada and freedom.

At this discreet establishment, which was notable for its disgusting food, Juliet and Esther remained for two years, attending classes in Arithmetic, Geography, Natural Philosophy, English Language and Literature, French, Latin, Continental History, Drawing, Vocal and Instrumental Music, Gymnastics, Botany and Italian.

Winnie and Freda were not sent away to school, maybe for reasons of health. But besides their home studies, Winnie and the others shared with the Tukes lessons with a Mr William Dawson. He was already an old man, the son of a cobbler in a neighbouring village. He had made 'a proper bad shoemaker', and finally took to teaching. He was entirely self-taught, or rather self-teaching; he was embarking on Anglo-Saxon at the age of eighty. Languages were his great love, and botany. Because of his humble beginnings he never fully appreciated his own gifts – but others did. He taught at some time or other in most of the Hitchin schools, and was employed privately at the houses of many middle-class families.

When Mr Dawson died in 1889, Esther wrote a memoir of him which was printed locally; and fifty years later she wrote in a nostalgic private letter:

> William Dawson was such a delightful friend of our young days and his old age; and living just across the street from our old home in Bancroft, he could share in the joys of the gardens and dell, with their birds and flowers, and the Hiz that ran through it so happily in those days, with kingfishers fishing in it and tunnelling their nests in the sandpits and the dell.

By the time she wrote this, the flowers, the kingfishers and the Hermitage gardens were already submerged by developers' bricks and mortar; the only traces of such serene times, and of William Dawson, were in the minds of his ageing former pupils. But in their young days old Mr Dawson was their inspiration – or at least, all that Hitchin could provide by way of inspiration. Meta said that he made the elements of Latin and Caesar's Gallic Wars an unforgettable delight. But, realistic as always, she adds 'but this was in part due to my own thirst for the waters of knowledge.'

This cooler assessment is probably fair enough. But Winnie knew how much she owed him, and she loved him. She ends a letter to him from Cromer in 1884:

> I like to think of you in the dell, listening to the wind in the trees. Take great care of yourself. 'Si tibi cura mei sit tibi cura tui': it was you who first taught me to understand and admire that line, you know. I wish I could show my gratitude for all you have taught me better than by being your affectionate friend, Winnie Seebohm.

*

In 1880, when she was seventeen, life began to open out a bit for Winnie. Being a Quaker, there was no question of 'coming out';

but she began to go away on visits, see new places, and meet people unconnected with the little Hitchin world. The Seebohm girls' growing-up process was accelerated by their mother's delicate health. The necessity for her to lead what was commonly called a 'sofa life' meant that the daughters took over some of her duties. Juliet from about 1879 frequently acted as substitute hostess, and was in charge of the Dinner Book, an exercise book in which she recorded who came to dinner and what they ate. (A typical dinner, given for Professor Vinogradoff in 1883, consisted of clear soup, cod, oyster patties, chicken quenelles, roast beef, partridges, corbeilles de creme, Victoria custard and cheese ramakins.) It also meant that one or other of the daughters very often took the place of their mother at Papa's side on his many visits to places and people of interest.

The first time Winnie went on a visit quite alone was to her aunt and uncle Barclay at their house in Brighton – one of their daughters, May, was about her age. On the first night away from home she sat up in bed and wrote Hugh an ecstatic account of the delights provided in the guest bedroom:

> Four boxes jujubes;
> One plate grapes;
> Two bone spoons;
> One tin biscuits;
> One glass coffee;
> One glass barley-water;
> Four blankets;
> One quilt;
> Two shawls;
> One fire;
> One hot-water bottle;
> Two maids to wait upon a poor creature who got rid of them as soon as possible!

In the summer of 1881 she and Freda and Hugh went again to the Barclays, this time to the Warren, their house in Cromer. Norfolk was rich in Quakers, and in summer they tended to descend on Cromer in droves. A Norfolk local historian, writing in 1885, noted that:

the place became a sort of rendezvous for a clan formed by the allied Quaker families of Buxton, Gurney, Hoare and the rest of them, who must be credited with great taste in discovering the beauty of the place, but whose invasion of it by no means tended to the general comfort of other visitors.

It is hard to understand how the Quakers, even in great numbers, could provoke such a hostile reaction – unless it was because they more or less took over all the best houses, the best beaches, the best servants, the best tradespeople, for the duration of the summer, as indeed they did.

It was here in Cromer however that Winnie made the acquaintance of the non-Quaker, well-connected Lockers (later Locker-Lampsons). She wrote to Juliet, who had gone to Germany with Papa,

> We have been much gayer the last day or two. Mrs Locker is very sociable, we see a good deal of her and her sweet children, and Mr Locker is very condescending and has read us a little bit of his poetry about meeting a goose on Ludgate Hill which dropped a quill and set him a-writing verses!

Winnie's impressions are sound. Mrs Locker would have been very sociable; Mr Locker would have been condescending. Frederick Locker, like Frederic Seebohm, was a man who in part owed his personal fulfilment to his wife's (or rather, his wives') private fortune. The son of the Civil Commissioner of Greenwich Hospital, he had not been a success in the position found for him in a counting house in Mincing Lane. Things were a bit better when he got a job as a junior in Lord Haddington's office at the Admiralty. Locker had some enemies, but none worse then himself. His anecdotes about himself convey his personality better than anything else could. He tells, for example, in *My Confidences*, of a long-desired boat-trip he had made as a child, about which he had been passionately excited beforehand. After only ten minutes in the boat, he said to his mother, 'Mama, why do people get tired in boats?' This feeling, he said, and this sort of sentiment, troubled him throughout his whole life. He suffered from chronic nervous stomach trouble:

Indisposition has made me nervous and restless; it has made me impatient and often weary of the subject under discussion.

And yet life treated him well enough. His first marriage, in 1850, was to Lady Charlotte Bruce, daughter of Lady Elgin and sister-in-law of Dean Stanley. Through her he met everyone who 'made their little fizz' as he puts it, in the social and literary world. He began to collect – books, objets d'art, people. He had excellent taste in all these – as somebody said, 'he sometimes seems to be *all* taste'. He published a collection of *vers d'occasion* called *London Lyrics*. These innocent rhymes delighted his friends and were fuel to the fire of his detractors.

But it is too easy to make fun of people like Frederick Locker. His preciosity and unease covered a desperate desire to please; and he desired to please because he had a loving nature. He disarmingly quotes his daughter Eleanor on this:

'You are always taking pains' she said 'about people who by disposition and taste are no way akin to you. You can never make them really congenial, however much you may efface yourself. You do not really sympathize with them, and they think less of you for the effacement, and for the very trouble you are always taking about them.'

In other words, he sucked up to people. Strong stuff from a daughter to her father. But his kindness and concern were genuine. When Winnie was in trouble the year after she first met him, Mr Locker was her great source of comfort. She spoke of him ever after as just 'he', with a reverent assumption that 'he' could refer to no other. Admittedly, he was extremely fond of young girls, and sometimes picked them up on trains; but he always put them down again. And he was a true friend to Winnie at nineteen with a broken heart.

But in that summer of 1881 when Winnie first met the Lockers, everything about them was new and exciting. Frederick Locker was now married to his second wife – Lady Charlotte had died in 1872 and within the year he had married Jane Lampson, a cheerful young New Englander, whose father Sir Curtis Lampson had been knighted for his part in the Atlantic Cable project. The couple shared with Sir Curtis his mansion in Sussex called Rowfant, which they inherited on his death. They also occupied on their own account a London home in Chesham Street, and a holiday house – Newhaven Court – in Cromer, which was where Winnie met them.

They were a splendid couple for a young girl to be taken up by, being intelligent, snobbish, rich and hospitable. This is how Winnie's first letter about them goes on:

> Mr and Mrs Caldecott (the illustrator of *The House that Jack Built* etc.) are staying with them, we are very interested in seeing him. He is very pale and delicate and apparently very shy. They also know Kate Greenaway and have asked her to come here but I am afraid she will not come. She too is delicate and suffers very much, drawing is her one delight and solace, and she lies on the sofa designing all those sweet little pictures until she is too ill to hold her pencil. Mrs Sam Hoare has called at last and asked us to play tennis there every Monday – so you may imagine how entirely she has won my heart! Sweet creature! Amiable soul!! Lovely woman!!!

With both culture and entertainment so admirably catered for, the holiday in Cromer was bound to be a success. Winnie went bathing with jolly Mrs Locker and her little boys. Hugh was 'getting some nice cricket'. Freda had a stiff neck. They grew quite at ease with the Lockers, and spent many evenings at Newhaven Court:

> We had a most delightful time, Mrs Caldecott and Mrs Locker both sang very sweetly (contralto). I like Mr Locker much better now. One does not notice his affected way of talking when one is used to him, and he is so kind.

One of the Hoare clan was being married from Cliff House that summer, and there was to be a dance from eight until twelve on the night of the wedding – 'I hope we shall go to the dance for a short time, but Mother has not quite made up her mind yet.' Cromer proved inadequate as a shopping-town for wedding garments:

> 'Just fancy!' wrote Winnie to Juliet, 'We could not get a pair

of four-buttoned gloves in Cromer! So we had to be content with two-buttoned, no very great calamity, but we *were* rather suprised at Cromer!'

So Winnie and Freda in their two-buttoned gloves went rather scornfully to the wedding:

The bride looked lovely and spoke beautifully, I think her voice could be heard all over the church; but even the Bishop could hardly catch the poor little bridegroom's gasps. It poured with rain all day, it was such a pity. We were to have gone to the garden party at 2.30, but as it had to be indoors we did not go until after 3. Then we sat about and talked, had ices etc, saw the bride go off at 4, and came away in a cab which required an umbrella held up inside, the rain came in so at the roof!

Mother managed to make up her mind, and Winnie went to the dance:

We went at 8 o'clock and stayed only till 10.30, but I enjoyed it immensely. Mr Sam Hoare was so very kind, he kept coming up to ask if I had a partner for the next dance and to see if my card was getting full. I must tell you more about my *first dance*(!) when you come home, and show you my card.

Winnie is eighteen years old – Winnie the Lion, Mary Ann's Moon-faced Chick. She is attractive, clever, critical, good at everything she turns her hand to. What can go wrong?

3

1882 is not there. There are almost no letters preserved from
that year until the autumn, and those that survive are only copied
extracts. Esther, who spent her maiden middle-age copying and
filing her family's correspondence, has obliterated the events of
1882. This kiss of death might have passed unnoticed, or as
mere chance. But there is one letter which, though mutilated,
escaped destruction. It is from Juliet to Meta Tuke, written on
February 5th 1886, about six weeks after Winnie's death. It
provides the only clue to what happened in 1882.

The letter is written on black-bordered double sheets. The
first two pages are mainly about the many condolences the family
have received. On the third sheet, at the bottom of the interior
page, Juliet writes:

> Now for my chief object in writing, which I have put off till
> last, because it is the most difficult. Do you remember there
> was something I wished I had told you when we were looking
> over her earlier letters? I hardly know whether it is right to
> let it go. . . .

The other half of the double sheet has been torn away. Baffled,
we pick up the threads on the next page:

> . . . . being guided by a Hand that saw further than we. She
> certainly would not have been strong enough to have met the
> strain of all that – neither the pains nor the joys of married
> life – it would have been like our Aunt Julia as far as our eyes
> can see into the future. She was just Winnie's age when she

died, you know, on the first anniversary of her wedding day. Could anything be sadder than that?

We heard nothing more till Christmas time, when he wrote a very touching letter. He said he had been very miserable for a long time, but had felt all along that Papa was right. His letter was very sweet to us because it was her 'goodness' and her 'rare refinement of mind' that he loved above everything. And he has been so faithful and so unselfish – and thinking chiefly of what was least painful for her too. He says 'It is three years since I saw her last, but I have not forgotten what she was then, for I have never seen her like. She has been a beautiful ideal to me ever since, and when I heard that she had passed away, a mist came over me'. There is no consolation in knowing that others are suffering too, and yet somehow it is sweet to know how tenderly she was loved, and how many others are missing her too. Three years ago I rejoiced in the thought of her with life before her, and imagined her choosing a path full of joy, and worthy of her, how little I thought that her happiness would soon be beyond my short-sighted judgment to influence!

What is all this about? The nameless 'he' of the letter, writing in 1885, said he had not seen Winnie for three years. Whatever it was then, it had happened in 1882. Evidently in 1882 Winnie was loved, and Winnie was in love. Her suitor must have asked Papa if he could marry her, and Papa had said 'no'. Why? The young man must have seemed unsuitable in some way. But to judge from the letter, he sounds to have been a paragon – 'so faithful and so unselfish'. Perhaps he was not a Quaker. Perhaps Papa thought Winnie was too young. Perhaps Winnie was not well; perhaps she had become unwell under the stress of family disapproval. But it must have been a very definite 'no', if the two never saw each other again.

And then the whole affair was as if it had never been. None of the next generation of Seebohms were ever told anything about it. The family correspondence for 1882 was later edited and censored. The half-letter from Juliet to Meta somehow escaped – though the page which no doubt gave the young man's name was carefully torn away. Secrecy is clearly the point of what Juliet was saying to Meta in that letter: 'I hardly know whether it is right to let it go . . . .' any further.

The conspiracy of silence was almost wholly successful. In the face of such deliberate obstruction, research takes on an indelicate and underhand air. The family did not want anyone to know about it; and in actual fact they have their way. It is impossible to say with certainty who Winnie's lover was.

Who *might* he have been? Somebody who never came to the house after 1882. Perhaps Juliet's Dinner Book will provide a clue. Perhaps there will be some name there around which to build a hypothesis.

The Seebohm's dinner-guests at this time were chiefly local or visiting Quakers – Tukes, Ransoms, Sewells, Pryors, Lucases, Barclays. They came mostly in pairs or en famille. But in November 1880 there was a new gentlemen guest who came to dinner for the first time on his own – a Mr Harley Rodney. He had a good dinner too; oxtail soup followed by sole, chicken, saddle of mutton, cabinet pudding and aigrettes de parmesan. He was there to dinner over and over again in 1881, either alone, or in company with the locals, or with the occasional visiting academic such as Oscar Browning. He was also present at the garden party that year, along with about a hundred and thirty other people. There are no dinner parties recorded for the following year, 1882, until October; Mr Rodney was not present then, nor is he ever recorded as having been present again.

It is worth following up. Who was Harley Rodney? He was well-connected; he was a descendant of Admiral Lord Rodney, and his mother was the sister of the first Lord Avebury. An only child, he was educated at Eton and Christ Church. The first time he came to the Hermitage he was just twenty-two, about four years older than Winnie. He had recently started work at the Public Record Office, and it is there that Frederic must have met him in connection with his historical research. But he must have liked the young man, or found him sufficiently useful as a research assistant, in order to invite him down to Hitchin. And young Mr Rodney must have got on well with the rest of the family, to justify the repeated dinner invitations during 1881, and to merit an invitation to come down from London for the Hermitage garden party in July. But evidently Papa did not like him well enough to accept him as a son-in-law. And Mr Rodney did not come to the Hermitage again.

In the 1890's and early 1900's Harley Rodney published some novels. Nobody can have read them for years. Maybe dusty copies are still propping each other up on the shelves of Edwardian country houses. From his novels a fairly clear picture emerges of the author's main preoccupations. They were love, music, idealistic socialism and social service. Winnie would have sympathized with all of these. His last two novels are stories for boys; at least, it is to be assumed that they are meant for boys. One of them, *A Treble Soloist*, is about a refined choirboy called Woggles. Details of the introits and anthems sung by Woggles are varied by accounts of his romantic attachment to an older choirboy whose exquisite treble has just broken. Woggles crashes the class-barrier: 'His clothes were common, his boots were very thick, and his tie was too bright; but I could not help liking him'. Later the two friends lie in the grass and discuss whether it is reprehensible to love one's best friend better than one loves Mamma.

Gummy's Island is a continuation of the same story. One of the choirboys discovers that his long-lost father is Lord of the Isle of Roses, a mediterranean paradise where slaves touch the floor with their foreheads as Gummy and Woggles walk by. But the boys miss their football games and their anthem-singing; they decide to come home and become good and useful Englishmen.

Mr Rodney's first novel – *Hilda, a Study in Passion* – is not to be mocked. Into it he seems to have put his most heart-felt writing. It is a pre-Lawrentian story about an inexperienced upper-class girl, Hilda, who is engaged to marry a man she likes but does not love. The couple have bought a house in Berkeley Square which they are having done up. While inspecting the work Hilda catches sight of a sensitive young builder's mate and falls passionately in love with him: 'His dark eyes, his soft voice, his clear complexion, his holland blouse!' On her second visit to the site she falls into his arms. His name is Charlie Palmer. Hilda visits a Mission in Poplar run by her fiancé's socialist friend Bernard, and there she sees Charlie Palmer excelling at football and chess with his working-class friends. Hilda and Charlie presently elope, and live in bliss in Normandy, where Charlie gets work decorating stately homes.

Hilda is the work of an acutely class-conscious person who is convinced that class-distinction is wrong. Harley Rodney can caustically dismiss one of his characters, Sappy Piggott, as 'the son of a ritualistic ironmonger who lived in a villa'; and yet the hero-figure of the book, apart from Charlie Palmer, is Bernard the Oxford graduate who rejects all class-distinction, lives in Poplar with the boys and is accepted as one of them.

Mr Rodney's narrative style is an exhilarating cross between Kipling and *The Young Visiters*. He is not a great writer. And yet there are one or two passages in *Hilda* that are worth rescuing from oblivion. When you remember that *Hilda* was published in 1898, it seems admirably perceptive and honest:

> In our northern country the physical sense seems to be dormant. Our educational system too is a perpetual lesson of self-restraint and suppression of the emotions. From the earliest age we are taught that it is cowardly to cry, improper to laugh aloud, unseemly to enjoy eating and feeble to love ease. Our whole nature is kept back, possibly guided and possibly controlled, only pent up to break out with irresistible force when the real overcomes the artificial and we act from instinct and no longer from thought. . . . Civilization is against nature and we are surprised when nature gets the better of the fight.

The only good reason for marriage, said Mr Rodney with the voice of his creation Bernard, should be 'sexual affinity'.

> We must either pretend to have no sex or attempt to suppress it. In most cases neither course is successful.

The man who wrote those things could well have been the man who was not allowed to marry Winnie Seebohm. Perhaps it was he – and perhaps not.

One thing is certain, and that is that Winnie was never quite the same again. She never recovered her careless optimism. In those miserable months she turned to God. She persuaded herself that the cruel separation was God's will as well as Papa's – indeed the two were inseparable. She was reading at that time Kempis's *Imitation of Christ* in Latin, in a paperback Tauchnitz edition. In Kempis's struggles she found a kindred soul, and copied out for herself the passage from *The Mill on the Floss* about

> the voice of a brother who ages ago, felt and suffered and renounced . . . and with the same passionate desires, the same strivings, the same failures, the same weariness.

She underlined the passages which were most apt to her own case; all the sad bits about doing without what you most want, nearly all the chapter 'De Obedientia et Subjectione':

> The greatest and indeed the whole impediment is that we are not disentangled from our passions and lusts. . . If God were always the pure intention of our desire, we should not be so easily troubled through the repugnance of our carnal mind . . . If God be among us, we must sometimes cease to adhere to our own opinions for the sake of peace.

Winnie is trying to be like the patient man 'who though he receiveth injuries, yet grieveth more for the malice of another than for his own wrong. For who is he,' St Thomas asks Winnie, 'that hath all things according to his mind? Neither I nor thou nor any man upon earth.'

And so Winnie sat alone at the little davenport in her bedroom, reading and underlining and struggling with what she was convinced was her worser self. She was only nineteen.

*

Late that summer Winnie was sent to the Lockers at Cromer. Mr Locker knew about her trouble and treated her with gentle sympathy. Winnie never ceased to be grateful to the Lockers for her kindness to her at this time. From Cromer she wrote long introspective letters to Meta, who also had problems. Mr Tuke had just remarried, and Meta found this hard to accept. The two girls corresponded at length on big subjects like faith and tolerance and goodness.

In this painful year Winnie and Meta grew analytical and began to clarify their intellectual as well as their emotional ideas. Winnie wrote from Cromer in September:

> What I think about knowledge (or rather about *mine*) is this: it is not so much knowledge I want as 'thought' and 'grasp'. It is no use knowing a lot of facts and truths if you do not know their relation to one another and to you. It is not enough to know the facts, one ought to know (and here I utterly fail)— the theories and thoughts of the person who tells one the facts, and one wants to work it all out for oneself, and draw one's own theories from the facts before one. I know the facts of the Norman Conquest alright, but I have nothing to say about it, because I have never thought it out for myself or mastered and compared others' theories and thoughts about it. Don't you agree with me?

We do. The historian's daughter is coming out into the light again. And 1882 ended with an event which took her, as she said to Meta, 'outside my little everyday world'.

The event was a visit to Tennyson, the poet-laureate, at Aldworth. The introduction was through Frederick Locker, whose daughter Eleanor had married Lionel, the poet's second son, in 1878. The lucky party consisted of Papa, Juliet and Winnie. This is how Winnie describes the excursion:

'Our long-planned visit to Aldworth has really taken place, safely accomplished without any accident, and got through without any snub. Papa, Judy and I started from here about 9 o'clock last Friday morning, and caught the 11.35 from London to Hazlemere. It was quite exciting watching the country turn gradually hilly, woody and brackeny. Arrived at Hazlemere we turned out and looked for the poet's lackey. We fixed upon one in red livery with a cockade in his hat, and marched up to him. He conducted us to a carriage in which were two big, strong horses. Not a very pretty turn out, we thought, but inside the shabbiness of the carriage surprised us. Neither of the windows seemed accustomed to be put up and one utterly refused. We drove through the little straggling village, with its amusing little houses and diminutive shops, and then out into the country. After about two miles we came to a gate. Hillo! The entrance to the estate, the poet's gate hath no lodge! And now we were climbing a hill, along a narrow lane, the hedges high and close on either side, no room to pass, mossy, ferny banks and sort of shooting copse and brushwood. Another gate, and we are out on a heathy moor, a splendid view, not the poet's estate after all, but a public lane, and now a public road over the moor, which is still considerably uphill. About another mile, another gate! and the footman now runs behind. Fine shrubs, gravel walks, lawns – the poet's garden! There are chimneys! The house! Not so very big! Oh no – the stables, and nice ones. Nothing to be seen of the house until a sudden sweep lands us at the front door, and the panting footman opens the door to us. We enter palpitating, Judy whispers something about fainting, tragic expectations. We are standing in the hall arranging umbrellas etc., on chairs. Sound of steps coming down the broad staircase – we all keep our backs carefully turned. I venture a side glance from the corner of one eye – it is a youth, not an aged prophet. Papa and he greet warmly, but Papa does not introduce us. After some hand-play, we *do* shake hands and are conducted into the drawing-room. Nothing to be seen but a large, broad sofa and on it a mass of silk quilt. Hallam says "My Mother", the quilt moves, and a woman rises, pale, thin and saint-like. She welcomes us very kindly and we feel at home with her immediately. Someone else comes in behind us and says "How do you do?" It is the poet-laureate!

'Hallam asks us to go upstairs, and conducts us to a pretty bedroom where a big fire is blazing. We undress, and find our way downstairs again. Entering the drawing-room, we find two ladies there, Mr Tennyson sitting by himself on the sofa reading the paper, Papa talking to Mrs Tennyson, who mutters something of which our own names are the only words we catch, and more hand-shaking follows. Then Hallam enters and proposes lunch. A pretty girl dressed aesthetically in brilliant green and having a mass of yellow hair falls to my lot. I cannot make my partner talk at all. The poet speaks never a word, and I could not dwell much on his countenance, for as soon as ever I looked at him, he looked up at me – we were opposite at some distance. Towards the end of lunch my pretty girl informed me that she had been at Cromer in the summer, and I thought "Come now, we can at least talk about that together", but she did not seem at all inclined to say anything more about it. After lunch we went up into the poet's study to admire the view, but he wasted all the time in looking up a word in Skeat's dictionary. That was all we saw of *him*, except that he came down to shake hands again as we were going away. He takes a nap after lunch.

So we trooped down again, and sat in the drawing-room and talked, until coffee came in, and then we departed. The pretty girl, we found out in course of time, was a niece of Mr Tennyson, and has married a Mr Pope who lives at Oxford. The other lady was Mrs Ritchie, we liked her very much. She came home with us as far as Vauxhall. We enjoyed our visit very much, though we were rather disappointed not to have heard Mr Tennyson *say* anything.'

There is an account of a visit to Aldworth in 1890 by Arthur Paterson which is strikingly familiar to Winnie's both as regards events – or non-events – and atmosphere. The Seebohms were not the only guests rather disappointed not to have heard Mr Tennyson *say* anything.

The aesthetic niece, whose name was Cecilia, was married to the Chaplain of Balliol. The other lady, Mrs Ritchie, was the elder daughter of William Makepeace Thackeray. Her sister Minny had married Leslie Stephen, and to start with they had co-existed in an uneasy *ménage à trois* in Onslow Gardens. Leslie Stephen found his noisy, impulsive, spendthrift sister-in-law rather a trial. He was even more appalled when after Minny's death Anne announced her engagement to Richmond Ritchie, who was not only her cousin, but her godson; and not only her godson, but seventeen years her junior. However, as Mrs Ritchie she prospered, and continued to write novels and to gossip and to pay visits; and she charmed most people, including the young Seebohms. Winnie was to meet her again.

4

1883–1884

In the spring of 1883 Winnie visited the Lockers again, this time at Rowfant, their country house in Sussex. She then returned with them to London, to their house at 25 Chesham Street, which was full of treasures:

> This house is bewitching. I feel inclined to spend the whole day in girating round and round the drawing room, to say nothing of pacing the passages and lingering on the stairs. You cannot find a square yard which does not contain something old or curious or interesting. It would take all Mrs Locker's writing paper to enumerate the pictures, china, old painted glass etc. which we have already seen, and I fancy that cannot be more than half what there is. Mr Locker has one bookcase full of first editions of Shakespeare and other dramatists before and after – other cases of old poetry and novels etc. This morning we are going to call on Browning, to which I look forward with horror!
> *Afternoon:* Oh! Mr Browning this morning was delightful, he *is* so kind and easy, and his sister too. His house is full of interesting things from Italy; and he showed us some things belonging to his wife, of whom he speaks a good deal. We saw the very chair in which she wrote *Aurora Leigh*! And her Hebrew bible with notes in her writing.

Elizabeth Barrett Browning had died in 1861.

Winnie was troubled all that spring by asthma and a sort of nervous coughing. The family were concerned about her health.

So shortly after her return from the Lockers in London she was off again, with Papa, Mother, Freda and Esther, to the Grand Hotel, Eastbourne, for a change of air. It sounds terrible. Freda got a stiff neck. Winnie wrote to Meta:

> In the morning Mother had a bath-chair and we strolled about. Then in the afternoon we had a victoria in which Essie drove with Mother on to Beachy Head, the rest of us walking there. Freda took Essie's place back and we walked round a different way, going past that great High Church Convalescent Home on the way back. I do not know whether it was getting tired that gave me asthma again, anyhow I had it a little last night, so have kept quiet today, doing the bath-chair with Mother whilst the others walked. The meals take a good while, as we have to go through with the menu. The food is far grander on the card than on one's plate, and the sauces are chiefly made up with lavender water and other scents. Our waiter is French and says 'I am not long here' when we ask him for anything off the menu.

But Winnie behind her daughterly behaviour was privately struggling to find a purpose for living. With quiet determination and periodical attacks of asthma, she inwardly makes her stand against Grand Hotels, bath-chairs and all their implications.

> 'I am quite sure,' she wrote at Eastbourne, 'that no woman (it is not my business to consider a man's life) has any excuse for living a life that is not worth living, and I am quite sure that every woman can find some work that she is fitted for.'

There was yet another holiday that year, in August. Juliet and Esther went to the Barclays at Cromer, and the rest went abroad with Uncle Henry, Aunt Maria and their ebullient son Ted who was at Brighton College. The large party 'did' Switzerland and Northern Italy, and all points between there and Hitchin. They looked at pictures and churches and lakes. Mother drank waters. It was all highly organised by the two Papas and Amato. Amato was the courier. He advised them on their itinerary, travelled with them, checked tickets, interpreted, dragged them up mountains and round galleries, poked about in hotel kitchens, and produced cold chicken legs from his fur satchel when he did not fancy what he saw. This did not stop all the Seebohms from getting stomach upsets. When Mother showed signs of flagging, they hired a donkey for her to ride during their excursions. 'Disastrous!' reported Winnie. The girls were rather overcome by the unaccustomed heat: 'Freda and I generally sport about in blue veils now, after having invested in a good deal of new skin' wrote Winnie, and again, on the way home: 'Freda and I have been holding a conference on the desirability of travelling in our cotton dresses, at least as far as Basle – or in our dust-cloaks minus a dress-frock, I meant to say!'

When they got home to the Hermitage in September, Winnie with relief took on some real work. She undertook to act as governess and give lessons every morning to her little sister Hilda, then thirteen, and Dora Ransom. Winnie took this responsibility very seriously, and spent a lot of time preparing the lessons and thinking of better ways of teaching. She had strong ideas about the way Geography in particular should – or should not – be taught:

Years ago, when I was young and ambitious (!) I began to write a new method of teaching it. But as that work has not been published yet, I have to put up with inferior ones! My governess duties are very delightful, we have been working just a week now, and I think are mutually satisfied with each other.

There was ever increasing work of another kind now. The Seebohms and other Quaker families in Hitchin had long been involved in educational projects and charitable works consisting mainly in visiting the sick and the old either in a private capacity or as District Visitors. Juliet took on District Visiting in 1883, and wrote to her friend Lucy Johnson, wife of a missionary in Madagascar, to tell her about it. Lucy in her reply points out the difficulty of doing such work effectively:

I in a cowardly way got out of the difficulty by not undertaking a task which I felt was beyond me; and indeed I was not at all fitted for it. But I suppose somebody must do such work. And if it has come to you, you will do some good I am quite sure. At the same time I think it is much easier when one has only natural relationships with the poor, when you get to know them gradually I mean, one by one and in a natural way. (This is a very incoherent way of expressing myself I fear.) I feel like you that it is difficult to interest oneself in poor people just because they are poor. And I don't really believe that anyone can really help anyone else, rich *or* poor, without personal affection and sympathy.

The educational aspect was perhaps more important. They worked through such media as the Adult Sunday School and the Hitchin Mechanics' Institute.

Mother subscribed to the Maternity Home and to the Girls' Training Home for Domestic Servants. Uncle Henry was prevailed upon from time to time to give ornithological lectures to the Natural History Club. Papa re-established the Grammar School on land donated by himself. He was treasurer of the Society for Bettering the Conditions of the Poor. He also conducted literary evenings at the YMCA. At one time he was reading them instalments of the *Idylls of the King* and the *Death of Arthur*. Unfortunately, according to the *Herts Express*, this little group was presently disbanded, 'but little interest having been taken in its proceedings'.

John Stuart Mill, Ibsen and the stirrings of socialism were on their side. But the Seebohms and other courageous people like them could not always bridge the chasm that lay between their own hot-house culture and the semi-literacy of their pupils. It is likely in any case that many of the middle-class Victorians who worked for the poor saw the education of the masses less as a tool for democracy than as a lever to boost their own laudable but private aspirations to 'goodness'. Their successes were no less successful for that. It was a beginning.

As the Seebohm girls grew up they became more involved in this sort of philanthropy. Juliet, the eldest, was the first to take a weekly class of working-men at the Adult Sunday School. In her absence Winnie took the class, one week in 1883:

I had eight men and they were very good and orderly, but I

found it rather difficult owing to the number of those who are mere beginners. I had taken great pains to prepare *Jephthah*. But there seemed to be no time at all for me to begin anything, we only read round about twice, and I found that summing up the substance of each verse took up quite enough time.

Winnie had rather an embarrassing time of it, for no-one would volunteer to start up the obligatory final hymn. 'The hymns really get worse and *worse*, I *do* think you ought to agitate'. However, she told Juliet that she thought the men were a very nice set. One Alfred Butterfield, indeed, was becoming quite gallant, 'and with a little washing he might pass for a gentleman'.

On another occasion when Winnie again took Juliet's class, a new scholar turned up. Winnie reported to Juliet:

I leapt up and beamed upon him, and your men gave him such a warm welcome that he looked quite happy and enthusiastic. He can read words of three letters, and has some idea of writing, tho' none of keeping to lines. They were all very nice to me and we chatted a great deal, chiefly about Egypt and Gordon. Do you know which of them has a brother out there? I cannot remember his name. At the end, Butterfield gave me a slip of paper he had found in his Bible, and I remarked that it was not *your* writing on it. 'No' he said, 'I know that'. 'So do I', said the one whose brother is in Egypt, 'it's too good for hers!' I wish you could have heard, and seen the sly look with which he said it, and the affection for you which was somehow conveyed in it too. The new boy's name is George Piper.

It seems likely that these sessions educated the teachers as much as the pupils. It certainly gave them a realistic view of current affairs. In 1884, after the fall of Khartoum, Winnie wrote to a cousin:

I am not a worshipper of Gordon. I am surprised to find from talking to our working-men who have relations in the Army that Gordon was not liked by the soldiers under him – they say he was so careless of bloodshed. We never did admire him as a whole – he was too mad – and that kind of presumptuous religion makes me shiver. His work amongst the poor and his endurance of hardship were very grand: but many are doing more at the first, and for the latter, it was no more than one expects of every Englishman.

The Seebohms were not apolitical. English politics in the nineteenth century were, as G.M. Trevelyan has said, as much a matter of denomination as of class. Political and social divisions remained very largely religious. The leading Conservatives in each town were generally the keenest churchmen. Their most active Liberal opponents were usually dissenters or anti-clericals. The Seebohms certainly fitted into this pattern. Papa was a dedicated supporter of Gladstone and the Liberals, and presided at meetings of the Hitchin Radical Association. Radicalism in Hitchin does not seem to have penetrated very deep. Winnie reports to Juliet in the summer of 1884:

Papa was at his working-men's meeting, in the chair. He was the only gentleman they had invited, and they call themselves Radicals!

Frederic's intentions were serious and he aspired to wider things than local politics. In 1884 he was planning to offer himself as Parliamentary Candidate for one of the Hertfordshire divisions. The forthcoming election was an especially interesting one, as farm-workers had just been given the vote – city workers had been voting since 1867. Winnie wrote:

The elections *will* be exciting – I do hope the people will behave well and not show themselves unworthy of what the Liberals have entrusted them with. I cannot imagine anyone really being Conservative in theory – progress *must* be the law of the universe!

In fact the new voters in 1885, the following year, did turn out for the Liberals, that is, against Squire and Farmer – another blow in the face for feudalism. But by that time Winnie was fighting another battle, which she was losing.

Before the elections came Papa was a disappointed man. His political career was nipped in the bud.

'Alas', wrote Winnie, 'Papa is not going into Parliament after all, which is a dreadful disappointment to him and to all of us. He is working hard now to help others in Hertfordshire – rather cruel work for him'.

The reason was that his partners at the Bank had decided that they could not spare him the necessary time away from his duties. This was rather unfair, as James Hack Tuke had been away for a good many weeks in 1882, for his work as Her Majesty's Commissioner for the Congested Districts Board in Ireland, administering his scheme for Irish emigration. But then Mr Tuke was the senior partner. The *Herts Express* said:

> Mr Seebohm has resolved not to offer himself as a candidate for any of the divisions of Hertfordshire, his business and private engagements preventing him from giving the necessary time that would be required for a Member of Parliament. Mr Seebohm during the last five years has created a very favourable impression, and his retirement will be generally regretted. There cannot be any doubt but that Mr Seebohm would have taken a conspicuous position in the House of Commons, and that he would have proved himself a most useful member of that august assembly.

In spite of political frustration and coolness in the Bank parlour, Papa's intellectual life was booming. His *English Village Community* appeared in 1883 and was received by professional historians with respect, even when they disagreed with his thesis. His main opponent was the Oxford historian E. A. Freeman, who could not stomach the idea that English freedom might be rooted in Roman slavery. Paul Vinogradoff however considered Freeman to be suffering from infantile and romantic racialism.

Paul Vinogradoff had entered the Seebohms' lives that same year. He was twenty-nine in 1883 when he first came to England from Russia to collect material for his thesis on English agrarian antiquities. He was a Russian giant, tall and bearded and powerfully built. On that first visit he only spent fifteen months in England, but managed to get to know all the Oxford and Cambridge historians. Maitland said that Professor Vinogradoff had 'the knack of making the right friends.' It was natural enough that Frederic Seebohm should be one of them – he and Vinogradoff were working, almost literally, in the same field. Vinogradoff came down to Hitchin several times to talk to Frederic. The two would pace up and down, up and down, their hands behind their backs, in their garden just outside the drawing-room window. 'Discussing the usual subject' supposed the girls, as they watched wistfully from the window of their sitting room on the first floor.

'The usual subject' bore fruit in Vinagradoff's case with his most famous book, *Villeinage in England*. He came back to England for good in 1903, to the Chair of Jurisprudence at Oxford, and was knighted in 1917. He and Frederic remained good friends until Frederic's death in 1912.

In the summer of 1884, the year following the first meetings, the Seebohms encountered the Russian bear again quite fortuitously on the beach at Cromer. Juliet made a sketch of the beard looking out to sea, and Papa took the opportunity of discussing his latest project.

Papa's latest project was rather curious. He had become interested in problems of metrology. He was trying, that is, to analyse the connection – and it seems he found one – between the various units of surface measurement used in the western world. Not surprisingly, his research consisted of measuring everything measurable.

Happily the project took him to Oxford after their return from Cromer, and he took Winnie with him. This is how she describes the visit:

We were staying with Dr Tylor, who is Professor of Anthropology there and lives close to the Museum. We saw lots of learned men, but they were all so kind that I had not an opportunity of feeling scared. We spent most of Saturday afternoon in the Bodleian Library, where Papa wanted to measure a lot of old manuscripts. Whilst he was busy with the others, Dr Tylor gave me a lesson in Anglo-Saxon from the *Caedmon*. Mr Freeman and several others came to dine with Papa, and as this was Papa's first meeting with Mr Freeman, who is so much against Papa's *Village Community* theory, it was very interesting. Mr Freeman was very charming and did not show any of his bearishness.

On Sunday we went to the University Sermon, then to lunch with the Warden of Merton [G. C. Brodrick] to call on the Vice-Chancellor. Then Sir Charles Dilke and Professor Fowler [Professor of Logic, President of Corpus] came to tea with us, and Papa dined at Balliol. Sir Charles Dilke disclosed the secrets of the Redistribution Bill to us, which was very exciting. But we are disgusted with the plan of single members, and all those horrid little divisions of counties and cities. Papa has been working hard for Proportional Representation, but now thinks it may have a chance in the next century! Sir Charles Dilke told us that *all* the Cabinet are against the scheme except Mr Gladstone, who thinks it right to give in to Lord Salisbury in that.

If these were exciting times for Winnie, they were exciting times for Sir Charles Dilke on a grander scale. This was November 1884, and Dilke and Chamberlain, the heavenly twins of the Liberal Party, were riding high. It was also exactly at this time that Dilke had become secretly engaged to the recently widowed Mrs Mark Pattison. He perhaps went on to call her at her house in Headington after having tea with Winnie and her Papa. Nothing, in the public or the private sector, seemed impossible for Charles Dilke at the end of 1884. But for him – as for Winnie – evil days lay ahead. In another seven months Dilke's career was to be shattered by the scandal linking his name with that of the silly young wife of the Member for a Lanarkshire division.

That same autumn also saw Winnie and Freda living it up in London. First they went to the Natural History Museum and to the International Health Exhibition ('tremendously interesting and exhausting'); and then, in somewhat unquakerly fashion, to the theatre, with Papa, Aunt Maria and cousin Ted. This was largely at Ted's instigation – Winnie describes his temperament as 'theatrical', and he was by now completely stage-struck and rather a worry to his Yorkshire mother. The play was William Gilbert's *Pygmalion and Galatea* at the Lyceum. It had first been performed thirteen years earlier, and Gilbert (and Sullivan) was already enjoying great success with the Savoy Operas. *Pygmalion* is Gilbert in an early, non-humorous vein. It was the first professional theatre Winnie had ever visited, and she was enchanted. She wrote to Juliet:

Ted sat with a friend, and was, I believe, most of the time in Harry Kemble's private room. The rest of us sat in the fourth row of stalls, exactly in the middle, so saw beautifully. The music was very beautiful, and was to me not the least enjoyable part. It *is* so nice to hear some violins sometimes! The theatre struck me as being very tiny, and very pretty and *very* proper. Miss Mary Anderson herself stands as the statue, and how she manages to look so stony and still I cannot think. The drapery looked exactly like stone too, yet the moment she moves it is the softest and thinnest of white muslins. It was all very beautiful, and it would take far too long to describe it properly on paper. Mr Terriss was the chief actor – and I liked him very much. It was over about 11 p.m. and we got home before 12 not at all over-tired or over-excited. Papa was much charmed, and Freda and I enjoyed it immensely. I was mightily impressed with the innocence of the whole affair – its simplicity, propriety and morality. I mean for the audience.

And then it was Christmas. That year the young Seebohms were performing a play, or 'getting up some acting' as Winnie put it,

for our servants, and the men and their wives, and then for a children's party afterwards. And as we make up the play, manufacture all the costumes, construct the stage, write the music, and act all the parts ourselves, this involves a good deal of time and labour. Hugh will not be home until Christmas Eve, so we are rather anxious about his part of the performance.

The play was a free version of Beauty and the Beast, or rather *Ye Beauty and Ye Beast*, a verse drama. Winnie played Beauty. It begins with Beauty and her sisters Gwen and Mab (Juliet and Hilda) mourning a dead linnet:

Gwen   We'll bury him kindly up in the corner,
        Bird, beast and goldfish are sepulchred there,
        Bid the black kitten march as chief mourner,
        Waving her tail like a plume in the air.

Mab	Bury him nobly next to the donkey,
	Fetch the old banner and wave it about,
	Bury him deeply

Gwen	think of the monkey,
	Shallow his grave and the dogs got him out.

Beauty	Bury him softly, flowers around him,
	Kiss his poor feathers, the last kiss, the last.
	He is quite dead, was dead when I found him,
	Plant his poor grave with whatever grows fast.

And so on, for three acts.

Hugh played the Beast, in brown-paper head and legs and sealskin gloves. For his transformation scene he astonished his audiences in red satin waistcoat, prune knickerbockers, and his Rugby cap.

Esther in a white beard played the Father, and Freda the wicked Wizard who put a spell on the Beast. The Wizard later proceeded in costume ('black gown with yellow serpents thereon, pointed hood, black stockings, and for a wand the gas-lighter, *lit*') to the Hitchin Infirmary, where she presented to each inmate three gifts from the tree 'consisting of useful articles'.

1884 was over. On the surface it had been a good year. Not many girls, Quaker or otherwise, had Winnie's opportunities for travel and education and acquaintance with public figures. But how was she, inside? Where was she drifting in her 'inner life'?

Earlier that year she had had her twenty-first birthday. She had spent it with Mother and Freda at the Glengarry Hotel, Bournemouth, and she had got asthma worse than ever before. Meta sent her as a birthday present a gold ring engraved with both their initials and the date. Sitting in the palm-filled lounge of the Glengarry Hotel, Winnie wrote to thank her, and went on with desperate earnestness:

Unless we *do* take our trials as from God, they must sour and estrange us, instead of drawing us nearer to Him. I too have felt lately as tho' I were coming out at the other side of the dark flood of doubt and perplexity and that God is there. And lately I have felt such a widened sympathy, as I have perceived how everyone is striving after the same thing in different ways, and often not recognising that it is the same.

Winnie wanted so much to 'be good', and yet was too analytical to be misled into thinking that it was a simple matter:

Indeed, there is no need for unhappiness to sour us if only we bear it in the right way. But I feel such a dread of growing narrow and hard, and it seems to me that some people, tho' they live a spiritual life, yet live it in such a narrow and limited way that it is only a blessing to themselves. I think it must be a want of faith that makes me in such a hurry to be up and doing. I ought to trust that when God needs me, He will open a way for me. I do not think the willingness will depart, do you?

The bonfires are burning. Winnie is longing to learn, and to be, and to act. But what can she and Meta do except be good daughters, and sit and wait? They did not wait very long.

5

1885

'It was in January 1885' wrote Esther the recording angel, 'that Winnie first made known her wish to go to Newnham. An alteration then made in family plans led her for the first time to feel that she could be spared from home. It is evident that her object in wishing to go was not mere enjoyment, but the desire to fit herself for possible usefulness in after life. As Hugh was going to Cambridge in October this seemed the natural time for her to begin too'.

Winnie was tired of waiting for life to begin. She decided to take matters into her own hands, and she wanted Meta to do likewise and come with her. Mr Tuke was away from home at the time, so Meta took the decision to begin studying for the Cambridge Higher Local Examination (the entrance qualification for Newnham) on her own and in secret. When Mr Tuke came home and was tentatively informed of his daughter's plans, he was not at all pleased. There were special reasons for this. Business relations between Mr Tuke and Winnie's Papa were rather strained, owing to Frederic's political aspirations and subsequent frustration. And Newnham, because it was undenominational, had a name for being the cradle for free-thinkers. There were quarrels and reproaches. It was finally decided between the two families that Winnie and Meta might study for the Cambridge Higher Local, to be sat in June. The question of whether or not they should proceed to Newnham would be decided in due course.

The idea of women at the University was not totally alien to

47

the Hitchin Quakers. Girton College had started its existence at Benslow just outside Hitchin, and intellectual ladies had been familiar sights in the High Street. Meta herself had retained from her schooldays a golden fantasy of a sunlit academic life. A teacher who had visited Newnham had told her of 'the green lawns where students walked and talked or sat under the trees with their books.' The child Meta had said to herself, 'I will go to Newnham when I am twenty-five.' In the event she went up two years younger than that, and stayed there, 'man and boy', as she put it, for twenty years.

What were Winnie and Meta letting themselves in for? What was the position of women in Cambridge in 1885?

Girton College was the child of Emily Davies. She was a firmly uncompromising feminist, determined that her young ladies should be regarded as *equal* to the men right from the first. She opened her College in 1869, choosing Hitchin as being equidistant from London and Cambridge and therefore convenient for visiting lecturers from either. She did not at first consider establishing herself in Cambridge itself – that would have been both dangerous and parasitical.

Newnham's beginnings were very different. There had been a movement for the higher education of women in the north of England from about 1867, instigated by the Ann Clough whose diary has already been quoted, and who found herself increasingly baffled and frustrated by the normal Victorian channels of do-goodery. The courses of lectures arranged for women in the north were crowded out, and the contacts made with lecturers from the universities helped the movement to spread south. Many distinguished people in Cambridge were sympathetic to the idea of higher education for women – among them J. S. Mill, Professor J. R. Seeley, Professor and Mrs Henry Fawcett, and, most active of all, Henry Sidgwick.

Henry Sidgwick was young and unmarried at the time, and it seems miraculous that such a person should feel strongly enough about women's education to take it upon himself to run a campaign. He was a good man and a clever one; the truth is that he was an advocate of reform in many areas of University procedure – he wanted to bring about changes in entry qualifications, in the syllabus, in the structure of the Tripos; admission for women was just part of the total plan, and the different causes helped each other.

'Lectures for ladies' were started in Cambridge, and Henry Sidgwick and his committee had a problem on their hands. Where to lodge the many lady students who would flock to Cambridge from outside? Obviously they would have to have a house. And someone to run it.

Ann Clough was an obvious choice, although her appointment was not seen in the first instance as the permanent post it turned out to be. Her work in the north was well-known. She had recently been meeting various influential people (Dr Jowett, J. A. Symonds, Dr Temple, Emily Davies) at the house of Mrs Samuel Smith, the aunt and slave of Florence Nightingale.

Miss Clough had been living with the Samuel Smiths since the death of her adored poet brother, Arthur Hugh Clough. Arthur had married the Smiths' daughter, although the young couple had never seen too much of each other since Arthur, like his mother-in-law, became enslaved to the iron will of the demanding Miss Nightingale. When Arthur died exhausted in 1861 it was natural enough for his sister to make her home with the bereaved Mrs Arthur and her family. But it was a stroke of luck that she did, because it was largely through the contacts she made in that household that in 1871 Henry Sidgwick lifted her out of a life of obscure dependence by asking her to take charge of the first five lady students in the horrid house he had taken for them at his own expense at 74 Regent Street, Cambridge.

The little group increased and moved house, increased and moved again, and finally launched an appeal that in 1875 built them South Hall (later Old Hall) at Newnham on land bought from St John's. North Hall (later Sidgwick Hall) was built in 1880, the two being joined by a public footpath.

The only examination the girls could officially work for during the '70s was the Cambridge Higher Local. This was originally set up for the benefit of Miss Clough's northern girls who had been industriously attending lectures and wished to prove themselves. Miss Emily Davies had rejected the scheme, for to her anything thought up specially for women was degrading, and would tend to keep down the level of female education. The continuing difference in attitude between Emily Davies and the more easy-going Newnhamites produced in Henry Sidgwick what he called an 'involuntary antagonism' – hardly surprising when he relates that Miss Davies accused him in a letter of being the serpent that was eating out her vitals.

But Miss Davies miscalculated the way things were going. What happened was that the Cambridge Higher Local Examination approved by Miss Clough turned out to be so satisfactory that it became in time the qualifying examination for both women *and* men who wanted to read for the Tripos.

Miss Davies' 'Hitchin College' moved to Girton in 1873. Women were formally admitted to the Tripos in 1881 – though they had no titular degrees for another forty years. However, by the time Winnie and Meta went up in 1885, Girton and Newnham were both on their feet.

But they were still only just tolerated. Only certain of the dons would admit women to their lectures. The girls had to go everywhere chaperoned, even to lectures. This imposed a most tedious duty on all the staff of the women's colleges from the Principal downwards. And 'Higher Education' was in many cases a misnomer at first, especially at Newnham with its gentle broad-based ideals. Girls' schools were mostly ineffectual in the extreme as far as academic achievement was concerned; Miss Clough had contributed a scathing paper on this subject to the School Inquiry Commission in 1869. Since there had been almost no means for a girl to acquire a serious education, the teachers and governesses were inevitably not much better informed than their pupils, and with few exceptions it was a case of the blind leading the blind. Girls who were 'educated' in any modern sense were either determined autodidacts or came from academic families.

The range of standards then in the early years of Newnham was wide: there were girls working for the higher Local Examination; girls reading for Tripos; girls not working for anything more defined than 'General Cultivation'; and girls who were not girls at all but mature women who had been waiting for years for something like this to be open to them. But this changed as generations of students left to become teachers and raised the standards in the schools; and by 1885 80 per cent of the students at Newnham were reading for Tripos.

Miss Clough the first Principal was not an academic. How should she be? The opportunities she was creating for others had not existed in her youth. By the time Winnie and Meta went to Newnham she was sixty-five and already rather frail. She worried continually about the health and happiness of her students like a fussy mother hen. She liked best the ones who had problems, and did not really care for girls who made it plain that they could look after themselves. With her 'vive la différence' philosophy she was in all ways the opposite of battling Emily Davies at Girton. But she generally managed to get what she wanted from the authorities even quicker.

She wanted to avoid at all costs acquiring an 'unwomanly' image for her college, and was terrified of the girls giving a bad impression in the Cambridge streets. Someone complained that Newnham girls had been seen hurrying along buttoning their gloves as they went. So Miss Clough admonished them gently:

'I know, my dears, that you have a great deal to do, and have not much time; but I don't like people to say such things about you, and so, my dears, I hope you'll get some gloves that don't need buttoning'.

Miss Clough's inclination for the personal touch was such that it is said that if she met one of the students going upstairs she would say, 'My dear, are you going upstairs?' And if she met a student going downstairs, she would say, 'My dear, are you going downstairs?' These attempts at contact, which irritated her more austerely intellectual girls, were the outward signs of a heartfelt affection for them all, which was generally gratefully understood; once when Miss Clough could find nothing at all to say to a passing girl, she kissed her instead – 'And I *had* been feeling rather depressed just then' recalled that student.

Whatever the shortcomings of the evolving system, the girls at Newnham could be sure of one thing in common – a serious sense of purpose and a strong character. It was no idle whim that took a girl to Cambridge. Only a very few hundred had gone before by the time Winnie and Meta went up, and, as Meta said afterwards:

A learned woman, a bluestocking, was a being held as apart from her kind. These Victorian bluestockings were not only learned. They claimed a certain independence for themselves, a recognition of their rights as citizens. A barrier was thus set up between them and the great majority of men and women among whom they lived, who were inclined to hold them in contemptuous awe. Many of these pioneers at the University entered upon their life with a sense of high vocation or noble enthusiasm. This was not my case. I entered Newnham as an Enquirer.

The high vocation Meta speaks of led most of the early graduates into teaching and into establishing the hard-working hard-hitting girls' schools which were to furnish the next and better trained generations of students. The other 'noble enthusiasm' was for social service, especially at Newnham, where right from the beginnings in the uncomfortable Regent Street house the girls had concerned themselves with the emancipation of their fellow underdogs, the working-classes, and had given lessons to groups of working men.

These few brave hundreds taking the first steps into a new way of life were freeing themselves, and indirectly their nieces (I would say their daughters – but an extravagant number of them remained wedded to their vocations) from the painful charade that the Victorian ideal of femininity had imposed upon so many women.

As Miss Clough said to her students: 'The world has become very interesting, it has opened out wonderfully. I think it is a happy time for women'.

This was the Newnham towards which Winnie and Meta began to work in the early spring of 1885.

*

An Honours Certificate in the Higher Local Examination admitted a woman to read for the Tripos without further preliminaries, just like the 'Little-go' for men. Winnie went in for the Literature and Languages Groups, taking French and German in the latter. Her sudden decision left her so little time for reading before she took the papers that she made up her mind to give all the time that she did have to the Literature, and just to do her best with the German and French. There were two Literature papers, each lasting three hours. The first was on English Language with special reference to the *Tempest*, Book I of Bacon's *Advancement of Learning*, and Addison's *Critical Essays*. 'This only requires the three above books to be learnt by heart and then you are safe, provided you understand every word' she remarked. Her other paper was on the History of English Literature with a special period, the reigns of Elizabeth and James I. 'Rather a *long* special period' thought Winnie.

She was appalled by the amount of superficial cram-work this all entailed – 'I think Newnham ought to be above that.' Hugh, who was working for entrance to King's, had an easier time of it.

Fancy! I find Hugh's exam is *much* easier than ours, tho' a certificate from his admits to the same privileges. Does it not seem unfair that, *besides* the disadvantages of our preliminary education, our inferior female intellects should be expected to do far more advanced work? My only hope is, that since these things are, as Cicero so prettily says, the standard of our papers can hardly be so high as the questions would lead one to suppose.

Meta was pinning her sceptical hopes on Theology – Hooker's *Ecclesiastical Polity*, Butler's *Analogy of Religion*, Paley's *Horae Paulinae*, and the *Book of Samuel*.

Besides all this cramming, the girls had to cope with the baffled disapproval of their less enlightened friends and relations. Winnie's cousin Ted, son of Uncle Henry and Aunt Maria, was of the well-worn opinion that too much learning spoils a woman. Winnie told him rather sharply that it depended what use she made of it. Ted sighed. 'Let's hope so,' he said lugubriously.

Winnie was still teaching her little sister Hilda and Dora Ransom in the mornings, and still taking classes at the Adult Sunday School. Her asthma returned alarmingly under all these pressures, and at the end of April she was packed off with Juliet for a change of air and a rest.

They went to Beach House, Freshwater, on the Isle of Wight. Meta joined them. They walked and read and botanised; Juliet sketched and painted. It was quite pleasant and rather boring. The boarding-house walls were covered with pictures of Tennyson and the food was predictable:

> The beef we had on Saturday is going to appear (for the last time I really do think) in the form of mince. We have already eaten it hot once, twice cold, twice in rissoles, and now once in mince !!! Total – six times. Some sea-weed enclosed for you to smell.

Winnie assured her mother that she was having good nights and felt 'quite another creature'. She needed more books, she had had enough sea air, she wanted to come home. And so after about three weeks' enforced relaxation she came home, apparently fully restored.

Meta stayed on a bit longer in Freshwater. She had been depressed as well during that spring, and was very low in spirit if not in health. After Winnie had left the Island she wrote to Meta from the Hermitage:

> When we are dissatisfied with our present condition *any* change appears preferable, but death is too vague and awful to be really welcome to any but those who look for the 'well done, good and faithful servant'. I often feel inexpressibly weary but I do not think *rest* is what young people long for, but rather work and power to work – fuller life and activity. I think work like yours and mine just now gives one rather a feeling of selfishness – the aim is so very definite and so entirely for our own immediate advantage. But then how often a man's business must seem so – and our final aim is not selfish. Of course happiness *is* what we all want, and what we cannot learn not to expect in some degree – but since it cannot be found by seeking, and since only a limited quantity is given to each of us here, it *does* seem wiser to leave *that* to Him who doles it out.

Winnie did not want to die. She wanted to work. If her asthma would let her.

For the exam on June 20th Winnie had to go to Cambridge – Meta too, but as they were being put up in separate places and taking different papers, they did not see each other. Winnie stayed with a Miss Kennedy, who was on the Newnham Council and was 'such a dear kind lady'. It all went off all right:

> I wrote hard the whole time without stopping a moment to think or weigh my words and only just got done in the time, so I felt very doubtful afterwards as to the result. If I had not been so very anxious to pass and so very doubtful of my abilities, I really should have enjoyed it all, because it was such fun and I like writing.

But her idealism was rather shattered by the non-scholarship required; she said self-righteously that 'you might have answered nearly all the questions without having read any of our great works'. There was a quarter of an hour for each question. The questions were extremely general – 'Give a short account of the Life and Works of Milton', and the same for Bacon. 'What *can* one say of *Samson* or *Paradise Lost* in a few lines?'

Winnie now wanted very much to do well. Hugh, who had sat his examination earlier, now knew that he was safe for King's in October. This was quite something. King's at that time was still very small – between eighty and ninety undergraduates – and the Etonian monopoly was only gradually weakening. Winnie and Meta had to wait in suspense until mid-August for their results.

But the waiting was made easier for Winnie by diversion in the form of a summer holiday abroad. They were all going, plus Uncle Henry, Aunt Maria and Cousin Ted – a party of eleven in all. Amato the courier was to accompany them again, and came down to the Hermitage to discuss plans and routes with Papa.

> Amato was here last night and said 'We *shall* be a jolly party!' It makes me realize that we are going, to have a sight of his bronze face!

Their destination this time was the brand-new Maloja Hotel

which had just been built right at the head of the Maloja Pass which leads from the Upper Engadine down into Italy. It was very grand and comfortable. The Seebohms enjoyed themselves. Winnie wrote:

There was an excellent Italian band belonging to the hotel which played most beautifully every afternoon and every evening, in a large hall which had a theatre at one end and a large polished floor. Twice a week they played nothing but dance music and then we had fine hops. There was such a lot of room that you could dance in real merry style, flying down the room and reversing and thoroughly enjoying yourself. But we liked it best when they played classical music, and we were so many that we could get up an encore when we wished.

Besides the eleven Seebohms the hotel was full of distinguished academic compatriots: Professor Max Müller, the great comparative philologist from Oxford, was there, whom Frederic already knew quite well. Max Müller himself wrote of this holiday, 'A most comfortable hotel, full of all sorts of pleasant people.' These included Mr Storey, a sculptor working in Rome; Mr Glazebrook, a Harrow master; Mr (later Archdeacon) Wilson, the Master of Clifton; A. J. Mundella, Radical Member of Parliament for Sheffield Brightside; and one or two Russian princesses.

In the middle of all this Winnie heard that she had got a distinction in both Literature papers, and second-class Honours in German and French. A note came from Miss Clough offering her a place at Newnham. Winnie had done it – and for her there was no question of turning the offer down. She wrote to her cousin in Australia:

Unless I go now I certainly shall *never* go to Newnham, and I have never in my life had any first-rate teaching. I shall, I hope, be more fit for teaching (or any other work) after a year or two of study there. And in my next I shall be able to give you a description of College life and the effects of 'Higher Education' upon the women of this generation !!

Winnie was wildly excited at the thought of her transformed future and full of exalted hopes:

> What I want to feel is that I am throwing my weight into the scale of advance, not the reverse. For each individual must either help or retard the final perfection, don't you agree?

Meta's application to the *Book of Samuel* had gained her too the offer of a place at Newnham. Until the last minute she found it hard to make up her mind to leave her father and her delicate sister Francie in order to do what she herself wanted. Winnie wrote to her from the Maloja Hotel:

> I *am* so glad your divinity is alright, tho' I always thought it *must* be in spite of your gloomy account. I am not going to say anything about your going to Newnham or not, because I must not bias you either way. Your circumstances are very different from mine. Of course no-one can go away from home without leaving *some* duties and making a break in the home life, but I think the question is whether the object justifies this – for myself I feel it imperative, and my success sweeps away the last doubt and hesitation.

And Winnie wrote to Miss Clough to accept the place for the coming October, and to Miss Helen Gladstone the Vice-Principal (daughter of the Prime Minister) to confirm that she would like to be in residence in the North Hall.

The Seebohms' fellow-guest Max Müller said on his return home that autumn, 'I wish we could have stayed at Maloja – I have never felt so well again'. We may wish the same for Winnie. Near the end of their stay she 'took a chill' and was very ill for a few days. When she was well enough to travel the family started home by easy stages, and though she seemed to recover her general health it was from this time that her sisters noticed the continual symptoms which became progressively less easy to ignore. The symptoms consisted of recurrent asthma and coughing which came on at night, and a curious constriction of her jaw and throat which on her bad days made it impossible for her to talk above a murmur or for very long at a time.

So it is that Winnie, declared totally restored to health after each and every little holiday of the last three years, is once more in a debile condition with only a month to go before she is to go up to Newnham.

*

She had always felt fine at Cromer. So that is where she was sent for a fortnight in September. She was to divide her time between her maternal aunt Mrs Joseph Gurney Barclay at the Warren and her more exotic friends the Lockers at Newhaven Court. The Lockers were now the Locker-Lampsons, and even richer, due to the recent death of Jane Locker's American father.

While Winnie was away Mother and Esther went to Cambridge in the rain to take a look at Newnham. Mother was not impressed, but Winnie refused to take her gloom seriously:

> I'm sorry that's how you felt about Newnham, you will have to come over again soon when I am there, and then I hope you will see it in brighter and more favourable conditions. No house looks nice when undergoing spring cleaning. Please thank Essie for telling me all about the rooms. The description of mine quite contents me.

Meanwhile at Cromer Winnie was enjoying the social life provided by Barclays, Hoares and Locker-Lampsons. Mrs Locker took great care of her and was determined to send her home blooming. Winnie in her letters assured her family as usual of her rapid and complete recovery. But she was not quite well. She found it hard to talk to strangers – 'jaw refuses'. She was happy and relaxed with the Locker children, whom she loved, especially Godfrey, the eldest:

> Godfrey and I played duets and then he said solemnly 'Do you know a Dead March? I love a Dead March.' When I was in the middle of it I was alarmed to hear him sobbing behind me, but he recovered before the end and thanked me enthusiastically.

This little boy grew up into a gifted man, a poet-politician. He went to Eton later, where he began writing poetry that was fiercely criticised by his father. After Cambridge and four years in the Diplomatic Service he entered Parliament and had a long and distinguished political career. And he continued to write poetry; *A Soldier's Book of Love Poems* came out in 1917. Besides verse he wrote books and essays on politics, history and art. In the years immediately before his death in 1946 he published at least half a dozen collections of lyric verse. That September afternoon in 1885 when he wept over Winnie's Dead March he was ten years old.

As always, Cromer was full of family and friends. Winnie's Barclay cousin May had just become engaged to Mr Claude Leatham. Winnie affected a superior disassociation from the 'spoony pair', though she agreed to be bridesmaid at the wedding which was to be celebrated the following January: a commitment that she was to be unable to fulfill. The engaged couple struck Winnie as 'quite useless' and giggled continually. Her apparent scorn of Claude seems however painfully ambiguous:

> The other night we had great fun guessing people's eyes through holes in a newspaper. It was such a joke when Claude did not know May's eyes from mine! Then we did little-fingers, it was so ludicrous. Claude and I are always having word battles, he pretends to think I feel my nose put out of joint and we are continually taking sly hits at one another. Really, what I have had to endure on the subject of Newnham and matrimony makes me rejoice at the thought of moving back to the Lockers tomorrow – tho' I *do* have to discuss both subjects up there too. When people are sarcastic I feel inclined to be the same, but I am afraid of hurting people's feelings. So I take it all meekly. People who are sarcastic never like it in others, I observe. Only when Claude joins in, I feel at liberty to give it him back. When he first came here I felt for the spoony couple but between ourselves he is such a mawly creature – his hands are always *on* somebody; if he reserved them for May I shouldn't think the worse of him for it.

Really Winnie must have been feeling rather better just then if she was up to such Games.

Luckily there was more to the Cromer visit than these back-handed sexual skirmishes. The Lockers' house as usual rang with the names – if not with the footsteps – of the great and famous. (Tennyson was expected, but did not turn up: 'Too stormy' he telegraphed.) Mrs Ritchie, whom Winnie had met at luncheon at Tennyson's house, was there:

> Mr Locker, Mrs Ritchie and I had a dear cosy little tea, and those two had a most interesting conversation about Thackeray, Tennyson, Swinburne, Browning, etc. It *must* be nice to know all those people really *intimately*.

Indeed ...

There were dinner parties almost every night. Augustus Hare, the travel writer and dilettante, was staying with the Lockers too, and was impressed by Juliet's talent for water colours. He had been looking through the visitors' book prior to drawing something in it himself, and asked who the Miss Seebohm was:

> and when I said, my sister, he said he had just been saying to Lady Darnley that it was the cleverest in the book, and beat Mr Caldecott outright, and that before seeing the name they had agreed it must be Kate Greenaway.

Augustus Hare did not however meet with Winnie's total approval either as an artist or as a man. She looked on while he sketched and painted the Cromer scene; and was shocked by the way he sacrificed 'truth' to composition and picture-making. She wrote to Meta that he was an excellent raconteur and very affable,

> and yet I have felt a natural antipathy towards him from first to last. I can only account for it by his way of saying rather nasty things about people, some of them *quite* untrue. He hurt my feeling the very first day by talking scandal of *dear* Dean Stanley [unconventional Dean of Westminster, uncle by marriage of Augustus Hare and brother-in-law of Frederick Locker by his first marriage]. And when I asked Mr Locker about it afterwards he told me he believed it was entirely unfounded.

When the fortnight was up she went home to the Hermitage

to prepare for going up to Newnham. The family were still worried about her health, and it was clear that there would have to be a doctor who knew her history on hand in Cambridge in case of need. It was decided that this was to be Dr (later Sir George) Paget. He was the brother of Sir James Paget, Surgeon Extraordinary to Queen Victoria. Lady Jebb, who lived next door to Dr Paget in Cambridge at one time, considered the brothers 'two of the ablest physicians in Great Britain'. George Paget was a lovely man. He was Regius Professor of Medicine at Cambridge, and during his tenure the School of Medicine was greatly improved and popularized. His techniques were considered progressive – he believed in detailed clinical examination of the patient, a procedure which may be routine today but which only the best men had got round to even by the 1880's. He had an eagle's face completely surrounded by whiskers; and is said to have looked like a preternaturally intellectual farmer.

It seemed that Winnie would be in good hands. Dr Paget came down to Hitchin to examine Winnie and to ascertain whether she was in fact fit to go at all. He pronounced that she was, provided that she did not work too many hours a day to start with, avoided stimulants, and got as much rest as possible. Miss Clough was to be briefed about her asthma and speech difficulties.

So on October 10th 1885 Winnie, Hugh and Meta went up to Cambridge with a quantity of luggage and a flurry of anxious sisters. Winnie coughed continuously on the journey. The sisters left, promising to come up again the following week.

Winnie was allotted a room on the first floor of South Hall, overlooking the garden. Meta was nearby in the room over the front door. They are very small rooms, but the windows are large and well-shaped. Each room has a doll-sized iron grate where the maids laid and lit coal fires every morning. Over the top of the doors were grilles for ventilation; the rooms were lit by temperamental paraffin lamps.

The closest friend, apart from Meta, that Winnie was to make among the other students, was Lina Bronner. Lina was one of the four children of Dr Edward Bronner, a German who had left his country for political reasons and settled in Bradford, which was also the first home of the Seebohms in England. There he joined the large and prosperous German community, of which he became an active member. Dr Bronner began his life of public service in Bradford by opening a small dispensary for the poor, which blossomed into the famous Ear and Eye Hospital which was built by public subscription in 1857. His daughter Lina had a lot in common with Winnie quite apart from their similar backgrounds, and the two girls were very strongly drawn to one another.

The two lecturers at Newnham who were chiefly to be concerned with Winnie were Alice Gardner and Mary Paley Marshall. Alice Gardner had got a First from Newnham in 1875, and had just returned there after a spell of teaching at Bedford College. She was one of the true pioneer generation. Winnie's adverse reaction to this particular type of 'new woman' was purely idiosyncratic but not incomprehensible.

Mary Marshall was quite different. She seems to embody all that was most romantic and idealistic about the first girl under-graduates. A rector's daughter from Nottinghamshire, she was one of the very first five students that Miss Clough came to preside over. She got a good result in the Moral Sciences Tripos in 1874, and when South Hall, Newnham, was opened the following year with twenty pupils, Mary Paley returned as the only resident lecturer at that time, to take over the teaching of Political Economy from the eminent economist Alfred Marshall, whom she subsequently married.

Though exactly how they achieved any real contact in that over-chaperoned academic world remains a puzzle. Mary Paley was invited to tea in Mr Marshall's rooms:

> A few suitable dons were invited and after tea we looked at photographs, which helped communication. Mr Marshall had a large collection of portraits, arranged in groups of Philoso-phers, Poets, Artists, etc.

But somehow in 1876 they managed to get engaged. And those days of the late 1870's, when Newnham was struggling to become accepted and the whole venture was still unthinkably exciting, those really were the dream days, the first days of the sunlit academic life which had fired Meta's imagination as a child. 'We papered our rooms with Morris' remembered Mrs Marshall sixty years later, 'we bought Burne-Jones photographs and dressed accordingly'. Her dearest friend was Jane Harrison, called the cleverest woman in Europe. Jane designed the embroidery for their tennis dresses:

> Hers was of pomegranates and mine of Virginia creeper, and we sat together in the evenings and worked at them and talked.

When Winnie came up Mary Marshall was thirty-five years old, happy and dedicated in her work and in her marriage. Winnie thought she was wonderful, which she was.

But Winnie was not long enough at Newnham to make many very close relationships. She went up on October 10th 1885 and left again on November 12th. The letters following are those she wrote during this time. Most of them are exactly as she wrote them, on small double sheets of paper with 'South Hall, Newnham College, Cambridge' engraved in black gothic lettering; some have survived only as copies or extracts in Esther's handwriting.

6

Winnie's letters from Newnham

Sunday 11 October: to Juliet
There is not much to tell you yet, but you will be glad to hear that I am not blown up yet, nor have I received any startling news from King's. I wrote a postcard just before going down to dinner, so I will continue from there. I am taken great care of at meals, being always called to sit by one of the fires – last night by Mrs Marshall and this morning at breakfast by Miss Clough. Directly after dinner last night there was a meeting to decide what papers shall be taken in and to sell the old ones by auction. What are not so sold, we have to pay for between us. As I was coming away, a Miss Mason[1] (a third-year student) asked me to tea at eight in her room, and when I said tea was a forbidden luxury for me, she said she had cocoa too, so thither I repaired and stayed about half an hour. My 'symptoms' call forth much sympathy and kind thought from everybody. When I was back in my room, Miss Clough called and stayed some time. Then I prepared my bed and was soon comfortably settled. They were having a cocoa-party next door, but I soon ceased to hear anything of them.

I had a most comfortable night and was called at 8.15 this morning, and just got down to 9 o'clock prayers. There were sausages and fish for breakfast and I took my cocoa down with me and made myself a cup with the hot milk. Cocoa is quite

---

1 *Frances Agnes Mason:* born 1849. Later Mother Agnes Mason, Founder and Mother Superior of Anglican Community of the Holy Family, for the Higher Education of girls. Died 1941.

fashionable here, and Miss Clough says she shall have some for breakfast as there are several other girls who would prefer it. After breakfast I sat in the 'blue room' until my room was straightened. There is a small library and a piano there. I went a little walk with Miss Athena Clough[1] (niece of the Principal) instead of going to any Church. She is very nice, and reminds me so of the Albrights with her hearty laugh and deep voice and broad figure. Then I reclined in my chair and read until lunch, and had another call from Miss Clough! Miss Athena knows the Lionel Tennysons and Mrs Ritchie.

Hugh came this afternoon, and we went for a walk together. I went to his lodgings with him and he left me to go to Chapel. His room looks so nice, and he had Green to begin on, and Bret Harte's poems! some of which he read to me. On the way back I met Miss Powell,[2] who is coming to see me this evening. Then I rested on my bed-couch till 4 o'clock, when I had an invitation to tea with Miss Athena. Miss Rickett was there too. She is very clever, did classics first, and came out Wrangler in Mathematics this year. Now she has come for an extra term to do the third part of the Maths tripos. Miss Sharpley[3], our classical lecturer, was there too. She is a little thin pale girlish creature – younger than many of the students, but when she talks and laughs she looks so nice and clever. I have just come back from there and now must get my letter written. It feels so queer, but my spirits are higher today, chiefly I think because I am better after a good night. It is cold today, but the sun has been streaming in upon me here. There is no fear of my not being warm enough in my own room, I have to put the door open when I leave it to cool it a bit. The ventilator over the door is very necessary if you do not have your window open.

Miss Clough finds that it *would* be more convenient for me to have my own bath – so will you send me one, or shall I *hire* one here? How nice Hugh looks in his cap! quite handsome. There is

1 *Blanche Athena Clough:* Secretary to the Principal at this time; she became Principal after Miss Clough's death.
2 *Margaret Powell:* The self-taught daughter of a Berkshire vicar, spent her life in teaching and education work in Newcastle. d. 1929.
3 *Edith Margaret Sharpley:* 1st in Pt. II of Classical Tripos, 1883. Tutor at Newnham for many years.

a little Dutch girl here, who matriculated at Cape Town and wore a cap and gown there, she says! Meta is looked upon by the new students as a sort of bath-woman, and has twice been called out of bed in the morning to the aid of distressed damsels struggling with a *full* bath!

Tuesday 13 October: to Freda

Your letter the other day was a great solace – I read it by the sitting-room fire, whither I generally repair after breakfast until my room has got quite warm and comfortable. Our letters are laid out on a table in the dining-room, where also is kept the book in which we have to mark ourselves as present. On Sundays we are marked at all three meals, I suppose that if I was absent at two an enquiry would be made, if at the third I was still absent a telegram would be despatched to you to ask if I had run away! Miss Clough is the kindest of kind creatures. The other night she lectured the students in her room on being late for Prayers, and then whispered to me '*You* needn't come down punctually, a quarter or half-past eight will do *quite* well for you!' As you can imagine, I am only too glad to take the extra quarter of an hour in bed in the morning! We may be as late as nine, but of course it is preferred that we should appear at Prayers.

I am beginning to feel more settled in now, though I still waste some time in making up my mind *what* to sit down to. The *social* duties are rather a burden to a poor dumb creature, and the proper 'calling' hours are just after meals so that I am more than ever unfitted for them, but I do as little of that as possible, and when all the old students have called on me, I shall be able to keep very quiet and exclusive. Tonight nearly everybody has gone across to the North Hall to a debating meeting. At the end of dinner Miss Clough rang her little bell and then said she hoped all students going to it would wrap up thoroughly this cold night and that those who had colds would not go at all. Then fearing lest I should not class myself in that category, she waited for me outside and said '*You* won't go, Miss Seebohm'. Yesterday as I was coming out from lunch she called me back and said 'Now Miss Seebohm dear, you aren't going to work, are you?' 'No,

Miss Clough, not just yet.' 'I should take a little rest after lunch, if I was you'. Which is what I always do. She also always either comes herself or sends a message by an old student to know last thing whether I am feeling alright for the night – I am generally preparing my bed when she comes.

Getting to bed is a matter of some time here. The sofa has to be converted into a bed, the cushions changing their hue from red to white; the bureau has to be cleared for a dressing-table, and books, blotter and pens exchanged for brush and comb, hairpins etc; the screen has to be removed from the washstand, and the towel-horse brought forth from its obscurity; and lastly the easy chairs have to be pushed against the walls to make room for the bath, which is brought in in the morning by a feminine duplicate of the lazy, cat-faced violinist of our Maloja band. To give you some idea of my days here, I will describe one to you in detail.

Tomorrow will be spent as follows, if all is well: I shall be called at 7.30, and go down to 8.15 breakfast, cocoa-tin in hand. If Miss Clough does not ask me to sit by her when I say Good-morning, I shall go down near the other fire, making my cocoa at the coffee stand. Then I shall mark myself in the book and look for my letters (and I hope there will be one!). At nine, muffled in several coverings, I shall run across to the North Hall for Miss Gardner's lecture on Constitutional History, *which* I don't care for much yet. I shall be back in my room soon after ten, and shall light my fire, get out my books, *take my medicine*, and sit down or recline with my books till twelve. Then I shall take some Brand's Beef (unless Mrs Marshall orders me milk and bread and butter downstairs) and go to Prof. Seeley's lecture on Political Philosophy. Hugh will be there, and I think of having lunch with *him* tomorrow. When I get back I shall rest, and go to 3.30 tea (or rather cocoa for me) with Margaret Powell. From four till six I read to myself or write my papers, and dinner is at 6.30 after which I do no work. At nine I make cocoa and am well in bed by ten. I have one lecture on Mondays and Fridays, and two on Tuesdays, Wednesdays and Thursdays, and none on Saturdays. Prof. Seeley's on Wednesdays are the only ones in the town. Most are with Miss Gardner, so I hope I shall like her better soon. Three times a week Constitutional History, and twice a week French History for which I am not going to read unless I have time begging. Twice a week Political Economy with Mrs Marshall, and I don't know yet how much work she requires, because she has a bad cold at present and cannot lecture.

So you see I am not working hard, and I don't know *why* I don't get quite well. Perhaps I shall soon. After all I've only been here three days, tho' it does seem *much* longer. I can't really tell you how I am, you must come and see me soon. That coughing made me much worse than I was when Dr Paget saw me, and I still have a fit of sort of nervous coughing generally soon after getting into bed. But I get out, wrap myself up and sit over my embers for a while and it goes off, and I get back to bed and sleep perfectly comfortably the rest of the night. All the first part of the day I feel perfectly well except at meals, but my jaw gets stiff and my tongue too towards evening. However, the last two days have not been so bad as Saturday and Sunday, so I hope it will go off in time. I only tell you this that you might not imagine my spirits *too* high and be disappointed when you see me.

Yesterday was sunny and pleasant and I enjoyed a walk with Meta. But today has been cold and windy and I have not been out since this morning's lecture at the North Hall. Miss Clough promises me a cab for Prof. Seeley's lecture tomorrow. She *is* so thoughtful of me, I could fill a letter with her little kindnesses.

I had promised to call on Miss Holman[1] after lunch (in the North Hall), but as it was so cold Meta took her my card with an invitation to 4 o'clock tea with me instead. I have done scarcely *any* reading this afternoon, for before I had finished resting Miss Rickett called, then Miss Rolleston[2] whom Dr Tyler asked me to meet at Oxford, and then Hugh came. As it was raining he had nothing to do, so stayed and chatted and looked at my work, and boiled the kettle for me! whilst I got out my biscuits, cakes and grapes. At 3.30 I went downstairs and fetched my allowance of milk and bread and butter, and we set

---

1 *Elizabeth Holman:* No Tripos. Later married, taught in Bury St Edmunds.
2 *Margaret Rolleston:* Daughter of Prof. G. Rolleston of Oxford. 1st in History 1886. d. 1929.

out a dainty tea. Meta and Miss Powell came too – I expect it was severely against the rules for Miss Powell to meet Hugh in my room! But I couldn't send either of them away. Miss Clough says *'if no-one is about* Hugh can *slip* into my room!!!' Luckily Miss Holman was rather late, so Hugh having finished his tea, he departed before she came. After Miss Holman and Meta went I washed some of my things so that Harriet might not have too much to do for a 'new student', and then got an hour's reading before dinner – and a visit from Miss Clough who is dining out.

Stubbs has arrived, thanks for it. A *flat* bath that could go under my bed would be more convenient. On Thursday I haven't any *lecture* after 12.30, but I have work that afternoon which I should prefer to do. Friday would be nicer, and Saturday nicest. If Mother can't come, can't *you* come? You haven't seen Newnham yet. Let me know in time to make plans with Hugh, and *do* come.

Sunday 18 October: to Juliet
I am spending this dull wet Sunday indoors, but I have just had the enjoyment of a visit from Papa and Hugh! before they go to lunch with Mr Bradshaw[1]. Bye the bye, concerning the latter, your advice (tho' always gratefully and humbly received nevertheless!) was quite unnecessary – I was only joking when I asked Hugh when he would take me to call on him! Please to remember that, like Tommy Big-Eyes, I am not *quite* a fool tho' I look it.

Miss Powell came over to see me this morning, and before her I received Dr Paget in cap and gown! He said Mother had written to him asking how I was, so he thought he had better come and see! This afternoon I have two invitations – to a tea-party at four o'clock on the next floor, to which I am not going, and to tea and paper-reading at 5.30, to which I *am* going as I shall not have to talk. Every Sunday some of the students meet like this in one of their rooms, and one reads a paper she has written on some 'Sunday' subject. Tonight's paper is on 'Kindred Spirits and Social Barriers'.

Last night I and two other girls were invited to sit in Miss

1 *Henry Bradshaw:* University Librarian; died the following year.

Clough's room and play the piano to her! It was very much out of tune but it is a happiness to get hold of *any* piano here, the public one is always engaged, except on Sundays. Another evening a Miss Villy[1] asked me to go and play on *her* piano, and that was a real treat, for she has such a sweet little German piano, and I don't feel shy of playing to *one* person, and we talked about music. She has asked me to go again on Monday. I have also been up to Miss Sharpley's room – I think I have told you about her, the little pale thin creature whom I took for a student at first, but who is the classical lecturer. She *is* so nice. She is now teaching a printer-boy Greek, so that he can set Greek types and so gain a higher salary. She has him up here in the evenings. Some of the girls too go into Barnwell to teach men history and political economy.

I am getting to like several of the girls very much, though unfortunately they are all third year ones! I haven't seen many of the people in North Hall yet – you see I don't go there after dinner as most people do – to political debates and dancing – so I don't make acquaintances on that side.

I was so charmed with all the things Mother and Freda brought, and so *much* obliged to you all for sending them. Dante looks so lovely and gives rise to much admiration and envy – as does Freshwater also. And the next time you see Cos. William,[2] will you please tell him that the chair *is* so nice, and that the first remark all my callers make is 'Oh! what a *lovely* chair!' I use it a great deal. I am glad you did not send me *your* candlestick, tho' I am deeply grateful for your willingness to do so. The screen is a great comfort, and looks well too; I thought it was to be for Xmas? The clock is invaluable, for my watch suddenly took to losing a quarter in every half-hour! So I was using one of Meta's, who has brought a clock and two watches! The other day I had half an hour between a lecture and lunch, so went a stroll down the road. Whenever I looked at my watch the time had not advanced more than a minute or so, and I thought I must be unconsciously walking at a tremendous pace. At last however I turned back and when I got in found how my watch was losing

1 *Florence Villy:* from Manchester. No Tripos due to ill health.
2 *William Ransom:* of Hitchin; manufacturing chemist and amateur archaeologist.

half the time! So now I take Meta's on important occasions, and mine is gradually recovering I think.

But now I must tell you about Mrs Marshall, from whom I have had two lectures. She *is* a Princess Ida. She wears a flowing dark green cloth robe with dark brown fur round the bottom (not on the very edge) – she has dark brown hair which goes back in a great wave and is very loosely pinned up behind – very deep-set large eyes, a straight nose – a face that one likes to watch. Then she is enthusiastic and simple. She speaks fluently and earnestly with her head thrown back a little and her hands generally clasped or resting on the desk. She looks oftenest at the ceiling but every now and then straight at you. She looks at Political Economy from a philanthropic woman's point of view, and talks to us each separately about the books we might read and the other subjects we are working at. We have got to write 'papers' for her too, which will not be easy, at least not for me who have read nothing before.

Yesterday I had a very idle day – one lecture in the morning. Then I read in the library for some time and really all the rest of the day I played! Before lunch I went a stroll by myself and gathered some red and yellow leaves to make my room pretty for Papa's possible coming today. Whilst I was arranging them in my room, with branches strewn all about the place, in comes Miss Clough and Miss Lowell, cousin of the poet, who is 'seeing over the College'. After lunch Meta and I went into town. After doing several errands together we parted, she going to the Post Office for stamps, and I to Hugh's lodgings for picture-cord to hang Dante.

As I was turning into Cat's on my way home I heard someone running after me, and there was Mr Lindsell who had been up here and found us both out. He came again later on tho', and had tea in Meta's room. Our little Dutch friend was in great excitement and rushed up to me explaining 'Miss Seebohm, you have a visitor!' 'Not I', I said, 'but Miss Tuke'. 'He *asked* for you' says she. 'I dare say', says I, 'it was Miss Tuke's brother-in-law, so he knows me'. When Meta came in she seizes upon *her* too; 'Miss Tuke, Miss Tuke, your *brother* has been to see you!' Which Meta did not think at *all* likely!

Mr Lindsell brought Meta some lovely roses, and to her horror, *more* cakes! The cakes that are heaped up under our beds are quite a nightmare to us! Meta was stuffing Mr Lindsell with as many as she could last night. We must try and give a tea-party sometime this week, I think, or else you will not be able to have *any* Cambridge fare at all!

I am looking forward immensely to having a visit from you, and Miss Clough asks me continually *'which* day is your sister going to come over?' Are all the days alike to you? I think Friday or Saturday would suit me best, but I will consult Hugh again and let you know. He will like to give you lunch, I know, and then either he could take you about and bring you up here, or I could come down and fetch you. It feels so nice and 'homish' to see the little man's face every now and then, and if only the weather would improve we might go some walks together. Cambridge looked *so* lovely the day Mother and Freda came, in mist and sunshine, so that the outlines of the spires and college buildings could not be seen quite distinctly.

Please tell Hilda I want to know how Mr Dawson is. And if anybody sees him, my love to him, please. How I wish I was quite well, there are such lots of things I should like to do here, and so many girls I should like to talk with. I find it best to explain my 'symptoms' to most of them, otherwise they think I am shy and try to draw me out! I don't much like the girl who is like me, tho' I believe she is clever. Would you like to meet anybody besides Meta? With very dear love and looking forward to seeing you soon.

PS. – Miss Clough always speaks of me to Meta as 'She'!

Tuesday 20 October: to Juliet
I went down to see Hugh this afternoon and we talked over Saturday plans. Hugh has no engagement on that day after eleven o'clock and will be delighted to give you lunch at one o'clock, and then show you the colleges etc. I will come down to his lodgings at 2.30 (you will have had an hour for walking about with him) and take you to *my* abode by Cat's and Queen's, and then you can look at Newnham and we shall have a nice time together and tea in my room. Will that plan suit you? Or can you

lay out the day better? I don't know what trains you think of coming and going by. My dinner is not till 6.30. I have found one or two more wants if you don't mind a *small* parcel? I want a bag for my linen to go to the wash in (quite a small one) and my napkin ring, please. And I should much like Chopin's Valses – we have two copies you know. The one which does not contain Freda's will answer my purpose.

I sat in Miss Clough's room most of last evening, and she sent for me again this evening but I said I wanted to write home. I *am* so glad Hugh is doing history too, it is so nice comparing lecturers and books. I wouldn't exchange Mrs Marshall for his economics lecturers, but next term I shall certainly go into the town for history. Yesterday was so wet and cold that I didn't go to Miss Gardner, so I had to go to her room in the evening to receive back my papers, commented on. And as I had feared she asked me who was my authority about the land-tenure! And I had to say 'my father'; she hasn't read his book and 'would like to look at it sometime'. It was excessively trying not being able to talk *then*. However she approved of the whole, and said it was 'very accurate and clear'. I have been at Adam Smith most of today, and I've now a paper on French history to do if I like. But as Guizot is already out of the library, and the subject is chiefly feudalism and chivalry, I don't feel very keen about it.

You *should* see Miss Gardner's get-up – droopy straw hat, shetland shawl thrown on without any grace, and big heel-less felt slippers in which she shuffles along. Then she evidently uses no mirror for her toilet, for this morning she came down with the ends of her hair sticking straight out like a cow's tail – she drags it back tight, twists it and sticks one hair pin through. The style of dress here is certainly *not* elegant – tho' I have hope for the future as most of the new students are neat and ordinary. Meta and I count the numbers of turned-down lace and stays – the former are numerous, the latter scarce.

There is a little German girl here whom I like rather – last night she came into my room and chatted to me. When she heard that I was working at history, she said 'Oh! is it your *father* perhaps who writes on history?' And she was so pleased when she found that it was. She told me she was so fond of the *Protestant Era* and began showing me parts that she 'read over and over again' – and said she wanted to read the *Oxford Reformers*. She comes from Bradford too, isn't it funny. Her name is Bronner. She has got a German friend from Hamburg to see her, who, when she heard my name, said she knew a Seebohm at Hamburg and had I an Aunt Rowntree!

There isn't time to write more tonight. My very dear love to all. Send Papa over here whenever you can find an excuse – a day's holiday so good for him, you know!

Wednesday 21 October: to Mr Dawson
Have you been wondering when I was going to write to you? I have thought of you so often, but my time is limited. To show you a little of what our life here is like, I will give you a minute description of today – only you must remember that most of the students are much more sociable and are also working much harder than I am allowed to this term.

At nine o'clock I took my books, muffled myself up in shawls and ran across to the North Hall where I go for history lectures from a Miss Gardner, who is not very interesting. *She* does not strike me as having her heart in her work or as being very enthusiastic in her subject – and you have made that a *sine qua non* in my enjoyment of teaching. Her lecture on Constitutional History, or rather I should say, on *Stubbs'* Constitutional History, lasted till ten. Then I ran back here, got my Adam Smith and read him in the general sitting-room till 11.30, when I went downstairs to the Paper Room and read The Times till Miss Clough was ready to take me to Prof. Seeley's lecture on Political Philosophy, which is held in the town near St John's College. Hugh was there too, so we exchanged grins as I went down the hall to my seat. I had to hurry back to my lunch so we only got nods and grins again coming out! After lunch I rested for about half an hour and then went out for a walk by myself. My next occupation was the making of cocoa on my own little fire and eating a solitary meal up there. From eight to ten most people have another spell at their work, but I am forbidden to read after dinner, so I am sitting in the sitting-room and writing to you. Sometimes I sit downstairs with Miss Clough, or in the library, or in my own room, and I go to bed very early.

At present I only go into the town for Prof. Seeley's lectures which are *very* interesting, but next term I hope to have my history lectures from the best men too. The lecturer on economics is a charming woman, I do not want to exchange *her* for a man. Every now and then I go to see Hugh in his quarters and sometimes he comes up here to see me. You know he is doing history and economics too, so we compare notes and books, it *is* so nice.

I haven't got acquainted with much of Cambridge yet, the weather has kept me in a good deal, and I find I soon get tired. How I should like to take a walk round the garden with you tomorrow morning. I have your face on my book-case, but alas! it cannot talk. Send me a few of your *written* words soon, to show that you haven't forgotten me – unless it is a bother to you to write. I hope Mrs Dawson is well.

Wednesday 21 October: to Hilda
I haven't forgotten the existence of my *fourth* sister, only I seemed always to have something particular to say to one of the others and I didn't care to send you a letter full of messages to them. Nor did I think it suitable to dilate upon my maladies to the youngest!

Harriet is becoming a very devoted attendant, and asks me now when she calls me what sort of night I have had and whether she shall bring my breakfast up. She amuses me immensely – she is too well-mannered to speak unless I address her first, but if I begin she is very loquacious, and pours out her troubles with Miss Tuke who is continually breaking her lamp chimneys. Harriet thinks she will be quite ruined if she goes on breaking three in a fortnight. She quite alarmed Meta by this suggestion so that Meta enquired humbly how much they cost – and learnt to her infinite relief and amusement, twopence each!

Mrs Marshall was as nice as before this morning, but she has given us a fearful paper to write – four long questions and we mayn't read up about them nor will she tell us anything about them till afterwards, we are to answer them from our own

Common Sense and by thinking them out for ourselves. Happily she doesn't mind a bit whether our conclusions are right or wrong so long as we *do* think them out to some conclusion. So this afternoon I have been sitting down to *think* for two hours, but alas I can reason most of them to two exactly opposite conclusions – a sadly unnecessary fertility of brain I have got!

This evening I have been at Miss Villy's piano again, playing to her and two other girls; not being able to talk makes me feel very musical. It is a way of expressing oneself I suppose. I feel so dreadfully bottled up, for most of the morning when I could talk a little I am at lectures or reading to myself.

Farewell for the present. Give my dear love to everybody – there are some things in Adam Smith that I want to ask Papa about, but can't now.

Saturday 24 October: to Freda

. . . We found Schubert's duets, presented to the College by some German lady, and after trying yours and mine we read new ones. Fancy, Meta could read off that march at the pace we got it to with infinite pains and weeks of practise. It seems hard that the same results should be gained with so little trouble! Tho' perhaps those who have had to expend much labour, gain in greater love for and deeper knowledge of what they must work at so much harder.

Today has been very enjoyable; I hope Juliet will give a good report of me. I had a better night again last night though the wind and rain woke me up several times. I have no lectures on Saturdays, so I worked at my Political Economy paper till eleven o'clock, then went into the market for some 'entertainment' for Judy. There is a dairy there, where they let you bring away cream in little tin cans to be returned when convenient. Then I went into a lane close by here to pick some fresh leaves for my chimneypiece. After lunch I rested, tidied up my room to look its best, put the kettle etc. ready, and then walked down to fetch her up. It *was* so nice having her, and I feel much better for it, both bodily and mentally.

When she had departed I went to Miss Athena to explain why

I hadn't been to tea and found Mrs Prothero[1] there so sat down with them for a little while. Mrs Prothero said that Mr Bradshaw has a very bad cold and is rather 'low', I think Papa ought to come over and see him !!!

I could not well be leading a quieter life, or one that I should feel more at ease in, I think. At this time of year I do not think I should be likely to get well quicker in another place, when I get out I am better – so if the weather improves I expect I shall advance in sympathy. I have not done any work since eleven o'clock today! No overwork you see! Very dear love to everybody.

Monday 26 October: to Esther

. . . The night was stormy and somehow I couldn't sleep properly, but kind Harriet discovering this, brought me my breakfast up so that I need not hurry down but might dress leisurely for my nine o'clock lecture. She is a good creature – a native of Norfolk I find.

I have been sitting chatting with poor little Miss Bronner who has a bad cold. She is immensely fond of Browning's poetry, so I told her of our call upon him. Her father is an ear-doctor of great repute in Bradford and has a large hospital there for the deaf and blind.

Breakfast is the least comfortable and homish part of the day, and letters just make me feel nice. You and Hilda *must* come soon. It's rather difficult to say just *how* far I have got – Constitutional History moves rather like a crab and slowly. But I think Henry II is pretty steadily in focus now, though this week's paper goes right back to Domesday Book and even to Edward Confessor. Hilda will envy me when she hears that I have to write a life of Harold Godwinson – but as it is only a fifth part of the paper, I don't much look forward to writing such a short one as it will have to be.

Miss Gardner evidently worships Stubbs – I nearly laughed this morning she was so funny. The lecture was on disputes between Church and State – chiefly Becket – and she said hurriedly

1 *Mrs Prothero:* née Mary Frances Butcher. Wife of George Prothero, Hugh's tutor – History Tutor at King's, later Professor at Edinburgh, and biographer of Henry Bradshaw.

and shyly after a somewhat lengthy pause (getting up courage I suppose for such an original remark!) 'The subject has lately been dramatized though that seems really unnecessary after Professor Stubbs' dramatic account of it' !!! In French History we are at Hugh Capet but it is very elementary and skimming.

I think the old students are beginning to discover that Meta and I are not schoolgirls. I rise in their estimation too, when such heroes as Mr Bradshaw ask after me !!

Winnie kept a memo book with an irregular record of her hopes and fears. The night of Monday 26th, after writing the letter to Freda, she wrote in her memo book:

2.30 a.m. My idea of heaven – a place where one need not *breathe.*

And on the following night, at 3.30 a.m.:

To those who are well and strong God reveals himself in the joy and beauty of nature, in music and colour, in the mountains, clouds and sea, and in the springing life of their own limbs and veins – but to those that suffer He reveals Himself more especially and more intimately in pain and weariness. At midnight when all else is still and silent, alone – wrestling with pain – then indeed one realizes as never before that 'There's nought in heaven or earth beneath, save God and Man'. Alone with God in the dark, facing death, then indeed is the soul's faith tested – either the 'everlasting arms' are there, or they are *not.* They are there. And their presence is burnt upon the heart never to be doubted or forgotten again.

The next day she wrote home –

Wednesday 28 October: to Juliet
It is rather late to begin writing tonight (for me, I mean) but I like to tell you how I spend each day, else I forget so soon any little differences between one and another. We have had *no* rain today and consequently I have felt better than any day since we came. Mother's letter at breakfast was a great comfort – tho' the account was almost too thrilling to be read in public. I am so sorry Hilda was driving, I hoped from Papa's account that

no-one else was there. Tho' of course it wasn't her fault at all. Still I dare say her young nerves will bear the shock more easily than some. Didn't the horse hurt itself? And must it be sold now? We *are* unlucky with those beasts! In fact cats are the only animals that do well in our establishment!

After Miss Gardner's lecture I worked till 11.30. Then had some refreshments and went to Prof. Seeley with Miss Clough. We came upon Hugh also bound thither and so we walked together. The lecture was very good. I walked home with a sister of Miss Rolleston who is visiting here in the College and whom I met at Oxford. I took her through King's, where I suddenly heard a well-known voice say: 'That's my sister!' and looking round saw Hugh walking with another undergrad. I think it may have been Fry.

After lunch Miss Sewell[1] called upon me. Then I took Mother's letter down to Hugh, who was just going off to his rowing. At four o'clock I went to tea with Miss Rolleston. Then worked in the library at the Charters. We have rather a nice paper this week, part of which is to show the grievances of the people during Rufus' reign from the Charter of Liberties granted by Henry I. I find the bad Latin of that period much harder to read than Tacitus and that sort – and a dictionary isn't much help! But that kind of work – making out the history for oneself as it were – is much nicer than describing the functions of the Curia Regis etc. from Stubbs. I try to show Miss Gardner the difference by taking pains over the former and writing long answers to them, and for the latter sort of hurriedly patching together sentences from Stubbs. But she criticizes so very sparingly that I don't know whether she doesn't prefer this after all!

After dinner I practised until eight o'clock then took my mending to Miss Bronner's room, for she doesn't work in the evenings either. We find many points in common – love of teaching, and of children. She is twenty I find, so not so much younger than me as I thought.

It feels queer without Meta tonight. I don't know whether it is to her absence that I owe a long visit from Mrs Marshall and

1 *Margaret Sewell:* b. 1852. Later Manager of Home Office Approved School at Buxton, Norfolk. d.1937.

then one from Miss Clough – which have hindered me in this. Auntie's pheasant came on Miss Clough's table tonight, and the breast thereof was sent down to me! Have we got a little Life of Bede, the 'Fathers for English Readers' series? I have lots more to say but must stop. Goodnight.

Thursday evening – another good day, my spirits are rising fast. We had such a nice time with Mrs Marshall this morning, she gave us back the papers and after the lecture stayed to talk to each of us separately about them. She *is* so nice. She and Miss Gardner occupied all the morning till twelve. When I came back here I found Meta had arrived and several packages in my room! Thanks so much for that jolly vase, which exactly suits my mantelpiece. And when you see Francie, please thank her too for the sweet little pots she sent me. It was so good of her. Meta had so much to tell me of everything. The bazaar sounds very successful so far. I hope you have had a good day today and are not too knocked up.

This afternoon I went a walk with Miss Samuels (of Jewish extraction, who is studying science here), we went to the Botanical Gardens, which were very nice, but it was cold. Since then I have been writing my 'Life of Harold', such a horrid hackneyed subject to give us! Who can say anything fresh about him – unless by original research which there was scarcely time for in two hours!

They are dancing at the North Hall again tonight. Miss Sewell came to dinner here – and we ate the partridges! Mother said something in her letter about coming over this week! I wonder whether *you* will. Perhaps you will be tired after the bazaar though. Meta says, if I come home Sunday after next, you won't come here next week – perhaps if asthma is wearing itself out, as it really seems to be doing now (getting less and less each night), it would be better to fight it out here and take my treat later in the term. I am not at all sure whether coming home for one night wouldn't be more tiring and tantalizing just now than it would be worth. But we needn't fix that yet awhile.

At first I put down all the new students as young – but I am beginning to find out now that a good many of them are at least as old as myself.

ABOVE All the buildings comprising the Hermitage, Hitchin

BELOW The Hermitage seen from the garden

LEFT Frederic Seebohm

*BELOW Mary Ann
Seebohm on the drawing-
room sofa*

ABOVE Winnie, Freda and Hugh

BELOW Winnie aged 13

BELOW Winnie aged 10

ABOVE May Barclay and Winnie (R) in a Christmas play, 1880

RIGHT William Dawson

Winnie Seebohm aged 21

ABOVE Hugh Seebohm aged 21

ABOVE Lina Bronner

BELOW Freda Seebohm

ABOVE (L-R) Esther, Freda, Hilda and Juliet in The Hermitage garden

BELOW Hilda Seebohm

Juliet's wedding, February 1891

Is Papa coming to the Greek Play? Miss Clough takes most of her students, but if Papa comes it would be so nice to go with him and Hugh. Give my love to Aunt Maria when she comes to you.

Miss Gladstone read *Tommy Big-Eyes* to her party the other evening, while they worked. She reads to them one evening in the week. Miss Villy's sister is coming to stay here next week – so you see *you* might come for a night sometime – tho' perhaps not till I am a more important person here. Miss Byles and I are going to the Fitzwilliam Museum one day soon – and Hugh and I to the Archaeological perhaps. I ought to be mending a hole in my stocking, so ta-ta.

Winnie's memo book, later the same night
To go steadily on in the path one has chosen, in spite of trouble, disappointment and even pain – how hard it is! How dark everything looks sometimes – all evil so possible, all good so unlikely. How one longs to give in – to struggle no more – but the will is still there, and reason knows that when the cloud has cleared away, the path will look as clear and right as before – and in spite of the weakness and weariness of the body – these two, will and reason, will not let us despair nor turn back from the plough. On the rack we cry for mercy, but with cessation of pain comes renewed strength of purpose and fresh determination to endure.

Friday 30 October: to Esther
. . . Oh! just think, I have broken two lamp chimneys! Meta is beginning to crow, but Harriet says I couldn't help it!

We all went across after dinner to the North Hall, the room was full. All the proceedings were amusingly formal and solemn. Miss Rickett was in the chair and looked so nice in a yellow silk frock. But oh dear! I *wish* I could describe the costumes to you! You never saw anything like it in your life! It might have been a fancy dress evening. Why can't I draw like Judy? The miserable attempts at Greek robes and hygienic dresses – I hope my new

1   *Mary Ann Byles* from Bradford. History Tripos Class II 1886. Friends' Social Worker. Married Alfred Maynard 1893. d. 1944.

Sunday frock is being made *very* neat and fitting – that is all I am particular about in it – nothing slouchy, bunchy or draggledy about it, *please*!

My idea of heaven – where one can converse without talking. I have often contemplated what it would be to be blind or deaf, imagined a life without sight or a life without hearing – both terrible but endurable I thought – the first more endurable than the second. But to be dumb – to lose all power of articulation, to be unable to ask for what one wants, to reply to kindness and sympathy, to express thoughts and feelings called up by every incident of the day – to be shut out from converse with kindred minds – *that* never occurred to me as a possibility, as a supposable form of suffering. It is hard enough to have no other means of utterance for the cry and the longing and the love within one, than *words*, at once so inadequate and so misleading – but not even to have *that* means! Oh God! Would not the pent feelings and thoughts burst the fragile body and escape? Debarred from human communion would not the soul take flight to Thee?

Sunday 8 November: to May Barclay
Thank you so much for writing to me amidst all the tiring work of packing up. I should think the weather quite drowned your grief at leaving Cromer, especially as so many others were leaving, or had left. It does seem such years since I was there with you all – teasing you a little and sympathizing with you a great deal. How strangely different the experiences are which come to us to make us grow! Your teacher has been love and happiness, and mine – his name is harsher but his hand just as tender.

Mother was here on Friday and took me to Dr Paget again; he says I am a little better, but I imagine from his manner that he doesn't expect me to mend very quickly. This is in answer to your enquiry – as a rule I think and say as little about it as possible. And I am so thankful he doesn't forbid my reading. I do thoroughly enjoy what little work I can do, and everybody here is so very kind. I think sometimes it is worthwhile to be ill or in trouble just to find out how much kindness there is in the world.

I have just been writing to congratulate Margaret Beck on her engagement, really one's friends are quite a nuisance when they once begin getting engaged – mine are going down like ninepins! It's quite refreshing to see so many sensible young women here courting Minerva.

Sunday 8 November: to Mr Dawson
Apologies are tedious, and yet I feel inclined to begin my letter again with one – but *you* kept me pretty long, until you don't know what suspicions and misgivings weren't coming into my mind! It may be that waiting for it made it more precious when it did come at last, but as a rule I prefer letters without that additional spice which is quite superfluous in my case – for your letters are always welcome, as you know.

Do you know I have *quite* forgotten Graham in *Villette*? so either your supposition that he is an attractive figure to the feminine mind is false, or my mind is not feminine.

Tell Mrs Dawson I forbid your reading *any* book for more than an hour. What you tell me about your ardour over that nasty botany book quite belies that line you so feelingly underline in the verse on 'old age creeping on' – if your mind is less prompt to meet a new study now than it once was, you must have been an awful person to manage in your youth! To be serious – I like what you wrote out for me very much and I wish I could read to you again, with all my heart. I sometimes wonder whether I shall ever be able to read aloud again – but it doesn't do to look forward, sufficient unto the day be the evil thereof, and the good too I believe, if we could only find it out. What a lot of good there is always lying round about us that we are blind to until something extraordinary opens our eyes to it. This is especially true in regard to the kindness and sympathy of other people.

I am beginning to count the weeks to the vacation. I long sometimes to see all the home faces, but I see them frequently and vividly in my mind's eye here – and I think about you all so much.

You are reading Herbert Spencer – I wonder how you like him?

Sunday 8 November: to Juliet
I have had three letters from the dear family since I wrote last, so I hardly know to whom to write this time, As I have begun to you, you must give my thanks to Freda for her kind thought in writing to me Friday night, it *was* so nice to get her letter the next morning. I hope her cold has quite gone by now.

There is a little person in the room, chatting away so lively and funnily that I really don't know how to write – she is just back from King's – where she 'has had such a horrid time' because the hymn was 'Just as I am' and she hates it; and 'everything sounds so sweet in King's that she couldn't help forgetting how she loathes that hymn'! And she is 'trying to read *Jane Eyre*' and 'revelling in Canon Liddon's sermons' tho' they make her dizzy when she has read a page because 'they are so difficult to understand but they're worth it because they are so grand and sublime!' She comes from the North Hall – very small and ugly and talking so excitedly.

Ah! now she's gone! and good riddance! And she was pouring it all out on the calm classical Miss Baxter!

Mother says she is hoping for a letter, but I hadn't much to say yesterday, and thought that with Hugh there you would be quite complete. My sentimental (in the French sense) side wishes to follow his example, but reason says much better go on quietly, and the time is going very fast.

Your committee sounds very amusing, tho' I fear the work is anything but that. What a pity there are not more Papas in the town – or why are *you* not a man?

I am sorry Mother gave such a gloomy report of me, *I* was feeling encouraged by Dr Paget's saying I was a little better. As long as he doesn't say I ought to be quite idle, I don't think I could be better off than I am here – reading and writing doesn't tire me so much as other things – and I am finding out now how much exercise I can manage. After being used to talking so much, it was rather difficult at first to realize the fall.

I hate the thought of the elections, and I hated the sight of Mr

Tuke yesterday – especially when, knowing that that would be what I should care about beyond all else, he began saying 'he had seen my father in the morning'! I should have appreciated the 'understandingness' from anybody else, but somehow it hurt me from him. It was like hearing Sam speak of goodness and unselfishness – it jarred.

Dear old Ju, I hope you will come again soon. I must wait until Meta comes back from Meeting to arrange about Wednesday.

I meant to have asked Hilda to look amongst our Brownings to see if *La Saisiaz* is there. Miss Bronner has it in a separate little volume, and I thought I might perhaps send it to Papa for his birthday if we haven't got it. Would you mind looking, and letting me know sometime soon please? I began one of Mrs Gaskell's novels the other day, but I don't get on very fast with it. I never quite like her somehow, tho' I can't discover why not. I think it's better to read novels in the holidays when your mind's not in other subjects.

Yesterday afternoon the Newnham Committee met; we were hurried over our lunch, the hall cleared and made smart, and then the Council discussed matters and were entertained with tea. I think some of the old students went in to tea, I saw Miss Athena go. But then she is somehow a *member* of the college, though I don't know why one so young is admitted to that honour, tho' her name *be* Clough!

There is a wretched girl here who sings your Schumann songs all out of tune – and another that plays the family 'Lieder ohne Worte' *so* badly – they nearly drive me wild sometimes. One gets quite callous to practising before people here, for it is so or not at all. Consequently those who don't care much for music drop it altogether.

Later: I shall be quite ready for Essie on Wednesday. Francie is coming, Meta says, at 12.30, and *she* will be in then. I am not out from my lecture till one, but shall be up here in time for 1.15 lunch with them, and then we can have a nice afternoon together, either in couples or quartette as we feel inclined! it will be so nice. *Five minutes to eight:* I have just been to tea with Miss Chamberlin, who has such a lovely room – so large and so prettily furnished. And such a big party – from the North Hall,

Red House and here. Miss Sewell was there. Then I have been down to Miss Clough, and since then writing letters. It is supper-time now. Mr Gosse was *so* interesting yesterday on Raleigh's minor prose works. He only lectures three times more, alas.

(Winnie's letter-writing was interrupted at this point by a visit from Hugh who had just been home for the weekend. He told her that the family thought she was too ill to go on at Newnham, and that she must come home almost at once. Papa was coming over with Esther on Monday, the following day, to arrange about her departure. They had already written to Miss Clough.

What happened in fact was that Papa came up alone on the Monday and talked Winnie into agreement. She actually left Newnham on Wednesday.

After Hugh had left her, Winnie finished her letter to Juliet.)

Hugh has just been up and I don't know what to think. Mr Tuke only saw me for a moment, so I don't know what he knows about me. And why be in such a mad hurry? I have so *much* to do to-morrow – and a lecture at twelve. There won't be any time to talk or do anything nice, if Essie comes then. Dr Paget *said* I was better, and I'm not working the least bit hard – and now I've got rid of asthma I shall get on. I *wish* you had written to me first before writing to Miss Clough and all – I can't bear to see her until we have talked and fixed, and it will just make her anxious – she will send for me to go down and I shan't know what to say. I shall be in between ten and eleven-thirty tomorrow but hope Essie *won't* come. And if Papa comes tomorrow too, it seems so unnecessary. Wednesday will be quite time enough, and it gives me time to think things over.

This is written in a great hurry before post goes. My spirits had risen after Friday's report – tho' they weren't low before by any means.

Winnie's memo book, late that same night
In case I should ever be tempted to regret my desire to come

to Newnham and doubt my motives, I want to write them down as I honestly conceive them.

My first object was to learn history well and thoroughly, that I might be able (should I prove capable later) to write it for the working classes.

Secondly, I thought after a year or two here I should be better able to judge whether I was likely to be capable of any work of this sort.

Thirdly, I hoped to learn here self-reliance, judgement and self-confidence.

I am quite sure that I never cared a bit about the examinations, and I do not think I ever counted much upon the enjoyments here – certainly not when I actually came. I looked upon the life here as the best preparation within my reach for the work which I hoped someday to spend my life over. And I thought it was perhaps as well that the enjoyment should be put out of my reach, for fear I might forget the definite purposes for which I came.

Monday 9 November: to Esther
. . . I was so glad to get your telegram this morning and then to see Papa. You must do just as you like best about coming on Wednesday. I think I should like to go to Professor Seeley's – but of course it won't much matter now whether I go or not, so fix as the family think best.

What I want to write now – because I can't *say* much of what I want to – is this: I am so grateful to *all* of you for taking so much trouble about me here, and sending me the things that have made my room so sweet and dear. My only regret in having come here this term is in your wasted bother and the money, but I *think* the latter would have to be paid even if I hadn't come – and I know Papa doesn't think of it. I can't think of anything more to say tonight, if you don't come on Wednesday I'll fix to come 2.15.

7

Defeat

So on Wednesday November 11th Winnie was brought home to
the Hermitage. Before Esther and Juliet arrived to collect her she
walked into Cambridge and bought some Christmas presents
and picture postcards of Cambridge to send as Christmas cards.

As soon as she got home she had a bad attack of asthma, which
was aggravated because of the very distressed state she was in
because of leaving Cambridge. In spite of her physical weakness,
she was tortured by the thought that she was missing Newnham
life. The day after her return home she wrote to Lina Bronner
and to Meta. To Lina she said,

> I have been thinking about you a great deal all day, I can
> hardly realize that I am not at Newnham. My mind still runs
> in the daily routine of lectures, lunch, work, dinner etc. You
> cannot think how queer it looks to see everybody so *leisurely*
> here! I wonder whether your family will strike you as exceed-
> ingly idle when you go home. It looks rather brighter this
> morning. I imagine you lingering on dear Clare Bridge, and
> King's spires will be looking grey and sharp against the sky.

And to Meta, who had written a letter to Winnie the very day of
her departure:

> I wanted to leave as much as possible behind me – it felt more
> hopeful somehow. At present it is my being *here* that is a
> dream – my heart is still with you, and I keep thinking what
> I *ought* to be doing at each hour. The meals come at such odd
> times here! You shouldn't say you can hardly believe I have

been, it doesn't sound at all well for me. I was flattering myself that one or two people knew that I had been! I think what you say is quite sound, and I shall try to take your advice – in fact I *am* taking it most thoroughly at present, for I seem to have come down with a run the last few days, like a watch with a broken spring, as soon as I put my work away. I suppose I was keeping my body up to my mind, instead of keeping my mind down to my body, eh?

On the Saturday after she came home Sir Andrew Clark came down to examine her. He was a fashionable and rather grand doctor. He was at various times Gladstone's doctor, and Tennyson's, Henry Sidgwick's and Alfred Marshall's. Mrs Marshall said that in 1879 Sir Andrew forbade her Alfred to knit – an occupation which apparently he found a great solace during convalescence. It seems that Sir Andrew was not an advocate of what would now be called occupational therapy; still less of what is now called psychotherapy, which was what Winnie really needed. But that wasn't Sir Andrew's fault – this is 1885. He allowed Winnie to knit, but not to do what she most wanted and needed – to read.

He reported to the family that he thought very seriously of her case, but at the same time held out a strong hope of her ultimate complete recovery. Only time, it seemed to him, could show whether there was any structural mischief to account for her difficulties with speaking and eating. Perhaps it was only a 'temporary affliction of the nerves' (nervous aphonia?) as the family were inclined to think. In the meantime he recommended complete rest of brain, and freedom from all excitement and agitation.

'Sir Andrew was very *very* nice (Scotch)', Winnie reported to Meta, 'and he amused me exceedingly by the way he put me through my tricks like a dog of parts'. But, as she told Lina, she did not at all approve of his treatment:

For in spite of this lovely weather, I'm kept shut up in the sitting-room, dosed and fed up (bah!) and allowed to look at *Punch* and the *Illustrated London News*! (bah again!)

For all her fierce words, Winnie did not make much progress.

Juliet noted how bravely and uncomplainingly she struggled with an ever-increasing difficulty in swallowing, and as one thing after another had to be given up, only liquids remained possible. Winnie showed no outward signs of alarm, only said sadly 'I shall have to starve soon'.

She was happiest sitting in the library surrounded by the beloved books, which doctor's orders forbade her to touch. In the evenings she sometimes joined the rest of the family in the drawing-room, for the pleasure of being all together. The descent from her precarious but independent Newnham existence to this almost mute invalidism was precipitous and bewildering. What was cause and what was effect? Nobody knew or thought to ask.

The arrival of the post was the highlight of her idle days, with the possibility of letters from Cambridge. Miss Clough and Mrs Marshall wrote, so did Meta, Hugh, Lina and other friends. Winnie put all her remaining energy into her replies, keeping alive (and being kept alive by) the passionate belief that she would return. In 1882 her own hopes and desires had had to take second place to family opinion; she had learned to batten down her frustration with 'Christian' resignation. Newnham had been her one chance to break through and take her place in life. Now she was back in the trap, and the closing in of the old tensions was to break her.

*

Sunday November 15: to Meta
After a little display of wilfulness I have got a pencil and paper just to occupy myself a little by beginning a letter to you whilst the others are down at supper. You will have finished your cold meat and no butter (how I envy you them) and be up in your dear little room again by this time. My thoughts have been at King's, and lingering regretfully on the bridges. I can see it all. The garden here looks very sweet, but I am condemned to stay in for a week, and 'to be made worse before I can be made better', which is not a lively prospect exactly! Don't ever bother to write to me when you've got work to do, or entertainments, but it *is*

so nice hearing from you, and every scrap of detail about Newnham and its happy inhabitants is water in a thirsty land. I am going to take a furtive glance at my little photographs soon. You can't think how difficult it is not to show them to the others, I do so want to give them the things I bought too – only I haven't quite fixed yet which is for which.

Monday: I can't remember what *you* do on Monday mornings – but it is Mr Gosse's last lecture, so Lina at any rate will be crossing Trinity Bridge soon after 1 o'clock. The trees are all bare here, except one little chestnut on the lawn, which still clings to a few yellow ragged leaves. I expect they have fallen visibly since I left, but that one outside my window was so thick still on Wednesday.

It seems a pity to have dismantled my room, now that Miss Herford is to sleep there. I am afraid she doesn't retire early enough for you to go and see *her* in bed by mistake!

Francie came up to see me yesterday. In the evening Papa read me one of Kingsley's Prose Idylls. There was one piece in it that reminded me of our last discussion. Describing the nightingale's song he says the only note of his which can be mistaken for sorrow, is rather one of too great joy; that cry, long, repeated, loudening and sharpening in the intensity of rising passion, till it stops suddenly, exhausted at the point where pleasure from very keenness turns to pain; and 'In the topmost heart of joy, His passion clasps a secret grief'. And do you remember in *Locksley Hall*, where the hero is thinking that to escape his keen pain he will give up seeking the best and highest, and live instead

Like the beasts with lower pleasures,
Like the beasts with lower pains?

I should have liked to hear about the Stoics. You see they had no ideal outside themselves as it were – so when they found it impossible to carry out their ideal in this life, they very heroically preferred to die; and in this light I agree with them. But our ideal is eternal, and when what we think the best way of attaining it is cut short, we have faith that yet another way will be opened to us. And that is why 'waiting' is service.

Monday November 16: to Hugh

I have just been enjoying thy letter, and feel it 'borne in upon my mind' to begin one in reply tonight, tho' I daresay I shan't get very far. It is indeed touching, and melancholy in the extreme, that letters should be passing between us again. However I've made a beginning there and I shall come back an 'old student' next term; I couldn't have endured to be a fresher when you were not! And it's better to have a break in *this* term, I opine, than in a later one. I have to summon all my philosophy you see to keep myself from pawing the ground and champing the bit and tossing my tawny mane! The dad is so sweet, too, that the hardest becomes easy.

Tuesday: Another lovely day, I have just seen Mr Dawson go down the garden, he is coming to see me soon. Minnie came yesterday and brought me some *lovely* violets, such monsters, and all cold and damp with the hoar-frost. The whole room is full of their scent.

I can see King's looking perfect this morning – the outlines all blurred with the haze, and all sorts of lovely little colours where the sun shines on the stones. Meta said she saw *you* in chapel – curious coincidence!!! Margie Powell read a paper on Sunday on the Stoics, which Meta says was very interesting.

I think Professor Seeley's voice *is* very comic, I remember he made us laugh in the second lecture, tho' I forget what over. Miss Byles is going to send me her notes, and I can see yours too at the end to compare and correct. Whenever I have seen other people's notes, they had got down some things so glaringly different from mine, that I shall feel safer with two sets. Papa says he encouraged your working – but don't get on too far ahead of poor little me! I am afraid you quite will in economics – and they won't let me read up here. Dear Mrs Marshall wrote to me, and offered to send me the papers they do, and to send mine back corrected.

Mr Dawson is reading *Eumenides* and says the Furies make his hair bristle, how I wish he could see it acted – wouldn't he be in raptures? I am afraid the excitement would be too much for him.

When you write now, remember no scraps of detail are lost on *me*.

Wednesday: Mother has just been up and says she's writing to you so I will finish this off to go too. I had a letter from my little German friend this morning – she has been to Mr Gosse's last lectures and says they were better than ever. Miss Clough thinks he will lecture again next term so I shall hear him some more. Don't forget the dad's birthday on Monday – I got Browning's last poem at Macmillan's the afternoon before I came away. I also got some little photos of Cam: that I look at fondly in private!

The men are going to have a chrysanthemum show, Judy has been painting prize cards for them. Lots of love, dearie, from thy sorrowing exile.

Thursday November 19: to Lina Bronner
I was so glad to get your letter – letters are a great solace. It seems like seven years since I left Newnham. If you ask me how I am – h'm – I'm as cross as a Kentucky cat. You were quite right about my making myself worse those last days – I did – and when I got home, collapsed altogether. That's the dark side – here's the bright one. Three sisters are my willing slaves (tho' very imperious nurses at the same time!), friends send me violets and roses, Papa comes up two or three times a day, and sometimes reads to me (something light and unexciting!) the window looks over the garden and the wood and hill beyond; and I'm knitting a pair of baby's socks to go to Madagascar. And Sir Andrew Clark said he would have to make me worse before he could make me better; so I hope the bettering process will begin soon.

So Miss Herford has been sleeping in my beloved room! If I had known I would have had the ornaments left out, I feel jealous for its honour.

There are three kittens in the house now; one which is perfectly black all over – not a white hair anywhere from nose to tail – was brought up to see me, and got loose, and wouldn't be caught, and a fine chase there was! Hilda calls him 'the little Wasserteufel' or oftener 'the Teufel', as being less objectionable than in English!

Do you remember our talk about some people not caring about

trees and flowers and birds? I thought of it yesterday when Miss
Tuke's sister Francie was here, and said she didn't want to go to
the Greek Play at Cambridge – her father offered to take her and
she 'hadn't the *least* desire to go!' And here am I wanting to go
so *terribly*, and now I don't suppose I shall be allowed to go. It's
a problem to me. I always want everything so *frantically*, and I'm
always *just* the person that can't have them! And I see lots of
other people who might have them easily and don't care to,
won't even take the trouble to put out their hands to take them,
while I am stretching out my arms lovingly and panting for them
and they are always hung out of my reach! Is there some great
lesson of life in all this, do you think? And ought I to have learnt
it by this time, and have given up wanting things? I've always
been like that, from my infancy; and now, after twenty-two
years, each disappointment is as keen – no, I think keener.

Forgive me for growling to you, dear Lina, but I can't show
it to any of them here. And if you know any solution to the
problem, or any numbing influence, tell me. 'Grosse Seelen
dulden still'; I try to, but one must have a safety valve, and I have
used my letter to you as one. Forgive me, and think of me when
you have time. My 'growl' you understand is not over the Greek
Play only, but over Newnham and things in general.

Sunday November 22: to Lina Bronner
Your spendid long letter was such a treat last night. I always
read my letters over and over till I cannot find anything that I
do not know by heart.

I quite understand what you mean about loving the *authors*
only I think one is so often disappointed. Can you realise that
Professor Seeley, nice as he is, is the author of *EcceHomo*? With
such a big double chin? I expected to see an earnest 'spiritual'
man, with a grave sweet face and far-seeing eyes! From his
portrait, would you ever have dreamed that music could flow
from Schubert? Jean Ingelow is the most common-place looking
old lady you can well imagine, and talks in a most common-place
way about common-place things. Even Mr Browning – as I have
told you, he was as kind and delightful as a man can be, but he was
not an atom like the creator of *Paracelcus* or *Sordello* or *La Saisiaz*!

94

I dare say Mr Gosse *is* conceited, though people often mistake honesty and freedom from false modesty for conceit. I know a man,[1] whom people who know him only slightly put down as 'very conceited', because he talks simply and honestly about himself and his own poetry just as he would about another's. Everybody admires his own work, he *must* or he would not give it to the world, but most people pretend to think their own productions trash, and simper when they are praised.

But to return to authors – and to poets in particular. What if the thoughts and emotions of *Paracelsus*, of *Aurora Leigh*, of the *Idylls of the King*, of the *Moonlight Sonata* are teeming in the souls of the whole generation of men and women; but to only one or two is the power given to express these thoughts and emotions, and put them into definite, living shape? Then those who are the voice of the generation will not necessarily feel or think more deeply or more nobly than their dumb fellows. They may even think and feel *less*, because they are able to find an expression – a beautiful and satisfying expression – for what is bursting their hearts. There are some whose lives *are* poems, who *are* music, and they have a still more powerful, though a less wide, influence in the world. Do you not know one or two people like that, whose mere presence thrills you?

One of the things I wanted very much to discover by going to Newnham, was whether 'knowledge' *per se* was really all-sufficient for some of the women of this age, or whether they were only trying to drown their hearts in it, as I half suspected both of them and of myself. I have not seen enough of them to judge yet. Some people are harder to approach than others, but I think very often it is just their outside crust, and right in their hearts they too are longing for affection and fellowship.

I think you're quite right about pain forming character – provided it's borne in the right way, for some people *do* shrivel up with suffering. But I'm not sufficiently clear about it, right now, to say much. The world looks very crookedly made to me today. I'll tell you what I think later on, when I begin to see the way out of my quagmire.

Miss Tuke has been down to see me, it was so nice hearing all

1 Frederick Locker-Lampson?

about everybody. Dear Lina, if you will write to me sometimes it will be a great solace. I should not mind the dullness now much, if I was sure it would not be for long, but I am haunted with the dread that it may really break into my work, and I cannot bear that! I am a coward, but I dare not ask whether I shall be well by next term. I must soon, but I keep putting it off.

Friday November 27: to Miss Naish at Newnham

How very kind of you to write to me! You are all so good to me that I really ought to be quite contented – though as a matter of fact it only makes me wish more that I could come back to you. I hope my exile is only a temporary one, but nobody is willing to say how long they expect it to last, which looks rather bad I fear.

All that you tell me interests me much. I should not like to have to speak on Bulgaria, though for a Conservative that would be a more agreeable subject than many. I am a Radical, though I should like to tie Chamberlain's head in a sack! But you have no need to remember my colours when you write to me – I am not rabid! And it is difficult enough to *talk* on political subjects, we won't try any discussions by letter. The elections are terribly exciting, all now depends upon the counties. I always feel so very sorry for the candidates who fail, we know so many and see so much of the work closely that I realize it all very fully.

My father and two sisters are coming to the Greek Play on Friday afternoon. Miss Bronner has sent me her notes on Mr Verrall's lecture. When I came away I expected to be able to come up to it, but they have made me into quite an invalid!

I am glad you find Miss Tuke 'good'. She has been good to me all her life. She is a sort of reed-bed to me, in which I pour out all my Midas-ears secrets! And we have shared all our thoughts and perplexities from the beginning of all things. It is queer how differently friendships are formed – some seem to be a sort of growing in to one another of the roots, so that however either of you may change, you never get further away from one another. In other cases there is a kind of magnetic attraction, and you run to meet one another without knowing why, and learn to *know* one another afterwards. Miss Tuke and I wonder sometimes whether, if we met now for the first time, we should like one another. We began by quarrelling!

My sisters read to me – Matthew Arnold, Browning etc. – so I am not quite given over to my own thoughts. I point out to them, when they enforce idleness too long, that if Satan finds mischief for idle *hands* (as we were taught in our youth, not unwisely) what must he not find for idle *minds*!

What a dismal day, I fear it is no better with you. In spite of all the rain we have had, in my mind's eye Cambridge is always lovely in sunshine, and King's Chapel smiling like a bride through its veil of mist. My father brought me Professor Fawcett's *Life* the other day, I see there is a good deal about his Cambridge life which will be very interesting to me. Biographies are considered just the right sort of thing to be read to me now. So the other day I tried to persuade one of my sisters to read me Mr Prothero's biography of Simon de Montfort, but unfortunately she was 'sure it would be too historical'! We have already been made to put by two books half-read, the nurses pathetically pleading: 'Well, we didn't know what it was going to be like, it *sounded* alright'! I have got *Stones of Venice* going though, which I hope will not be stopped.

Saturday November 28: to Meta
I have been looking out for that woman who was going to stand for some London district,[1] she seems to have collapsed without any explosion. Papa thinks the sheriff would have refused to accept her nomination, but very likely she did not carry it as far as that. Poor women! It's sad to see them going astray like that, and casting their pearls before swine, but it isn't altogether their fault. I know something of what drives them to it. If I had the genius of a novelist or poet, I would write a book to show it all, and try to point out the right pathway to them – and to make men see them as they are a bit. I have the plot in my head. Perhaps after three years at Newnham – sh! For I *quite* mean to stay three years now tho' we won't mention it yet.

Judy is painting some Christmas cards, such pretty ones. She

1 Miss Helen Taylor, Parliamentary Candidate for North Camberwell. On Nov. 24 she attempted to hand in her nomination papers three times, and was turned away each time.

suggests my taking to painting now! I tell her I'm too vain – or too artistic.

There was a letter from Sir Andrew Clark yesterday, saying I might walk out as much as I liked, so I am glad and triumphant. They had been talking nonsense about bath-chairs and waiting for sunshine!

They are blistering the back of my neck now, which does not exactly conduce to comfort either by night or day.

Tuesday December 1: to Lina Bronner
What a nice day for you again! Everything here looks so pretty in the sunshine and white dew. I have been a walk round the garden, with a sister on each side. Crossing *our* little bridge, and looking at the reflections of our leafless trees in the pond!
Friday: The last few days I have been out driving, and as they don't like me to write letters in the evening, I seem to have had no time for finishing this. It feels so long since I saw you – if I don't come back before June you will have to stay another year!

Was it not good of Miss Naish to write to me? Dear Miss Clough has written too. I wonder whether Harriet has had better news of her grandfather, I have often wanted to know. Have you seen the December *Nineteenth Century*? There is an interesting paper by Huxley replying to that one of Mr Gladstone's which we read together. So you are going home on Tuesday now? You lucky girl, I wish *I* was going home next week!

Thursday December 3: to Meta
I sympathized so with the parliamentary candidates in their suspense yesterday,[1] and indeed, I have been feeling deeply for all the failing candidates in Britain, just think, if *we* had not got into Newnham? We know what it is now, to be racked with suspense and to contemplate settling down to one's ordinary life again in case of failure.

I have been thinking too how probably many of them were obeying what seemed to them a call to work for God – and they

1 Polling Day Dec. 2nd.

will be suffering with my pain! Indeed the pain of interruption in earnest work must be a very common form of suffering, only I never contemplated it before. In the only cases I knew of, the men had so many strings to their bows, possibilities in them for so many great works. After all a *man* can always find work, it is much harder for a woman to find work – that her family will approve of. But I am trying not to think about work. 'Wait thou upon the Lord, commit thy way unto Him and He shall give thee the desires of thine heart'.

(Winnie's asthma was getting worse not better, and no improvement could really be expected in other ways while she was so continually racked and exhausted. It was suggested that the low-lying situation of the Hermitage was to blame. William Ransom, whose daughter Winnie had taught, and who had lost his wife earlier in that same year, suggested that she might benefit from the higher ground of his house, Fairfield. On December 9 she was driven to Fairfield from the Hermitage, and installed – rather unimaginatively – in the big front bedroom that had formerly been Mrs Ransom's. The change had an effect in that she enjoyed at least two asthma-free nights. But there was no improvement in other ways.)

Thursday December 10: to Meta
I have been meaning to write to you each day since getting yours, but have not been up to it. I have been having such violent asthma these last few days that I have been made worse than ever, and was almost in despair. Cousin William has been so kind as to invite me up here to see if the higher site will do good, so I was brought from my bed up here, in the shut carriage, and I had a rather better night last night. I am up now, and thought writing to you would take my mind off my miseries a bit. My hand seems rather feeble, but I hope you can read this.

Is it not sweet of them to have such a troublesome visitor?

Juliet has just carried off my soup to keep warm, that I may 'try again soon', so I replenish my failing powers by writing to you.

They have galvanized me several times – once it really seemed to do good. I had a horror of it at first, through superstition or ignorance I suppose, but it hasn't hurt yet, only feels rather eerie.

It is very touching being in the room where Cousin Anna Mary died, where I saw her shortly before her death, and again lying in her coffin so pure and lovely. I think it must be rather painful to Cousin William to have all the invalid appliances brought in to this room, and to come and sit with me here – but he is so good and kind and unselfish.

Saturday December 12: *to Lina Bronner*
I am afraid I cannot write very much or very legibly, but I must send you an apology for a letter, or you will think I have forgotten you, now that you are safely landed in the bosom of your family once more. I have been rather bad the last few days, but have taken a turn for the better again now.

Dear Lina, I have given up all hope of coming back *next* term. I see that no-one dreams of it, though really I cannot grasp it, my rebellious heart cries out against such a cruel decree. But the hand of God works inexorably and takes no heed of our cries of pain. It has been very hard to recognize His hand in this trial. But I am trying hard now to think that He has some lesson to teach me first, and certainly if it is in preparation for the future work that is my single aim, He must prepare me in His own way. So, if I can keep hold of this faith, my suffering is reduced to personal loss – my new friends and pleasures missed, and a time of some pain and weariness to be borne.

(The effort of getting to bed that night after putting aside her letter brought on a severe attack of gasping for breath with fits of violent shivering, which went on all night. Her sisters watched aghast and Papa sent for Sir Andrew Clark. But when he arrived the next morning he found Winnie apparently recovered and relatively cheerful. When he had finished examining her she sat up and completed her letter to Lina, making no reference to the fearful night.)

Sunday: I am in bed today so you must excuse pencil. About Professor Seeley's lectures – a babe could understand them, but

I think they only serve as recreation, like Mr Gosse's. I suppose you would not like to join Mrs Marshall's class in economics? Or very likely your science will be quite enough. Biology is a subject that always attracts *me*.

We are not to act this Christmas, and have made very unstable plans as yet. I employ myself in making Christmas presents. No more now, dear Lina.

Sir Andrew spent the rest of Sunday with the Seebohms, and looked in on Winnie two or three times during the day. The fact that her symptoms did not seem aggravated by the strain of a totally sleepless night made him more than ever hopeful of her recovery. He seemed to think it would be a good idea if she could get right away from Hitchin fairly soon for a complete change of air. He departed towards evening, leaving everyone, including Winnie, immensely cheered.

Sir Andrew had said that she might now do 'anything she liked, in moderation'. At once she asked her sisters to bring up her Euclid from the Hermitage, and also Ruskin's *Stones of Venice* which they had put away after a few chapters, considering it too heavy for the invalid. Winnie also began to make detailed plans for a programme of work to be done at home until she could go back to Newnham.

She had by her at Fairfield the exercise book she had kept at Newnham for writing memoranda to herself. In it she now indulged her obsession with Cambridge and her Newnham room, with its view over the garden and tennis courts, and the thick leafy creeper that tapped against the panes: 'such a little Paradise!' She was thinking too of Mrs Marshall, who had found the way; who chose to find no conflict between her independence and her feminine role: 'If *she* is the woman of the future I am sure the world will do very well, and wives and mothers be much better than they have been so far.'

The last entry in the book is an extract copied from the *Pilgrim's Progress*, which Winnie had always loved, she said, for its 'quaintness and vigour':

I am a man of no strength at all, of body nor yet of mind: but would if I could, though I can but crawl, spend my life in the pilgrim's way . . . but this I have resolved on, to wit, to run when I can, to go when I cannot run, and to creep when I cannot go. As to the main, I thank Him that loves me, I am fixed: my way is before me, my mind is beyond the river that has no bridge, though I am as you see.

On Wednesday of that week Winnie wrote to little Oscar Rowntree in York, all about kittens and pigeons and going to school. And this is how Esther, with a detail characteristic of her generation, describes the following day, Thursday December 17:

Before getting up Winnie was bright and cheerful as usual, but whilst dressing the gasping for breath came on again. It was relieved for a time, and during the middle of the day she resumed her usual occupations, chose Christmas presents for some of her little friends, and enjoyed being read to as usual. Whilst struggling with the difficulties of swallowing her last meal, a little book of Mrs Ewing's was read to her, to which she had been attracted by the motto:

> The courage that dares
> And the courage that bears
> Are really one and the same.

Early in the evening the struggle for breath began again, with other distressing symptoms. This attack did not respond to any remedy that there was to hand. It lasted nineteen hours – all through that night and through most of the next day. Winnie, wrote Esther, though in acute distress, never lost control. The worst thing was the repeated disappointment of relief, as everything possible was tried and found useless.

They sent a telegram to Sir Andrew Clark, but he was unable to come down.

The final remedy (tincture of opium?) used in compliance with Sir Andrew's answering telegram, sent her gently off to sleep soon after two o'clock, still sitting in the same position, her head resting on a table before her, as she had been all the weary hours since the evening before. She did not wake again. After two hours of peaceful sleep and rest from pain, she gently ceased to breathe, at about four o'clock in the afternoon of Friday, December 18th 1885.

Winnie was buried the following Wednesday in the burial ground of the Society of Friends. The reading was from Corinthians I, the second part of the fifteenth chapter: 'The last enemy that shall be destroyed is death'. The grave was lined with evergreens and white chrysanthemums. 'The coffin' reported the *Herts Express* 'which was of polished oak and made by Messrs Allen and Barker, was covered with beautiful wreaths of white flowers'. The *Herts Express* also made the observation that the late Miss Winnie Seebohm was 'a young lady of winning manner and amiable disposition, with a remarkably matured mind'.

*

Winnie died and life went on without her. It was not a merry Christmas at the Hermitage that year. On the last day of 1885 Esther wrote in the back of her diary:

> This, the saddest tho' not the most unhappy year of my life, has taught me that no real evil can befall those who with single aim seek the good, because to them all obstacles become stepping-stones; the greater the obstacle, the higher they mount. So that the only thing to be dreaded in this life is the being weary in well-doing, or falling away from the strife, or losing sight of our aim. Also this: that whatever one may learn is only to be kept by living it out. The love I feel will go if I do not spend it. I think the highest aim within my reach at present is to give as much happiness as I can to those close round me. This includes the cultivation of my own mind to my utmost power. My great obstacle is selfishness but surely this too can be triumphed over?

In January Hugh went back to Cambridge and performed the depressing task of calling on Miss Clough and collecting the things that Winnie had left so hopefully at Newnham. His work helped him to get on with his own life, and so did his tutors. Professor (later Bishop) Creighton had him to dinner and talked him out of a depression. 'One thing he said' wrote Hugh to Freda, his favourite sister, 'that struck me as especially true, was that emotions that do not really drive us on to actions are degenerating'.

Hugh continued to enjoy Cambridge; that year he rowed for King's, and began to learn to play the flute. But there continued to be occasional bad moments. On February 14 he wrote, again to Freda:

> There was a strange mist so that you could not see across the King's quad [*sic*]; not even the outline of the opposite buildings. I wandered out on to King's Bridge and stood there some time. The water was only just to be seen and looked white and cold. I always go there when I am gloomy. And then my thoughts wandered to last term. And, as if in answer to my thoughts, Miss Bronner went by to a lecture, alone.

In our time British people are apt to cope with grief by burying it. The bereaved, after a short interval, must be distracted and cheered, and prolonged unconcealed mourning is unhealthy – even inconsiderate. In 1885 people still dealt with grief by indulging it, letting it take over completely for a while. This led to temporary emotional prostration and to some bad literature; and maybe to a more real understanding and acceptance of loss.

After Winnie died the grief-machinery started up at once. Juliet and Esther sent photographs of Winnie to Miss Clough, Mrs Marshall and to Harriet, the Newnham maid, as well as to all the relations and friends. They wrote to all Winnie's correspondents asking them to return any of her letters that they had kept. From these they copied in triplicate a set of extracts which they circulated among friends and family, along with a detailed account of the manner of her dying. The passages they chose were the most edifying and 'spiritual' ones. And the events of 1882 were erased in the authorized version of Winnie's short life. Juliet wrote to Meta:

> If there is anyone you would like to lend them to we would willingly let you have them. We have overcome our first feelings about not liking them to go out of our hands, and

they are so inspiring and purifying that we *like* anyone to have them who will read them with sympathy. I thought your cousin's (*entre nous*) rather a cold little note, didn't you? It made me wish she had not asked for them, but perhaps I am wrong. I think it is true – the more I think of it – what someone has said, that her life was perfect in its incompleteness; and so many besides ourselves find the little they know of her so inspiring that indeed we cannot but feel that 'the good die not'. Nellie Barclay says she thinks of Winnie when she feels impatient under her sufferings. It seems to me that the darling is doing a greater work than she ever dreamed of, and if her letters are a help to anyone, we should be selfish to keep them to ourselves. Only we don't like the thought of them in *print* as so many people want. It seems to take away from the sacredness of them.'

For the family, everything concerned with Winnie was now 'sacred'. By editing and sanctifying Winnie, Juliet and the others helped themselves to bear having lost her, and that was good. The image of Winnie that they made was a beautiful thing, and it was the truth; Winnie had been all that they said she was. But their image of her was only part of the truth. She had been a person of enormous potential, both of mind and heart. She was a born giver, a life-enhancer. And because of pressures and circumstances and conventions it all came to nothing.

Nobody could have been more loved in life than Winnie. But it is a sad fact that the love of parents, brothers and sisters, is not enough to give life a shape for most adults. Winnie was the victim of a system: there were hundreds in the same predicament before her, and it is still happening all the time. Mostly the victims smoulder on, but Winnie's bonfire was completely doused. Winnie died.

Why did she have to die? Her asthma killed her. Why did she have such asthma?

*

Physicians since Hippocrates have understood that asthma is a psychosomatic illness. That is, in medical terms, that the inability of the patient to cope with the circumstances in which he finds himself sets up an emotional disturbance which translates itself into a physical disorder. The twentieth-century connection of asthma with 'allergies' only adds yet another link to the long chain that joins emotional protest to bodily protest.

The sort of emotional conflict that might result in an illness such as asthma is seldom due to one single cause, but is rather the outcome of a combination of circumstances. Yet it is possible to generalize discreetly.

Studies of asthma patients have shown that they have generally been overprotected as children, with a dominant parent to whom they are particularly attached. It could perhaps be said that the Seebohm children were overprotected – many Victorian children were. The little Seebohms were at any rate most tenderly cherished, and protected by Quakerism, wealth and snobbery from many of their Hitchin neighbours. Their adoration of Papa was evident and maybe inevitable. Frederic Seebohm certainly instilled into his children a very developed sense of family solidarity, call it what you will.

Overprotected children are inclined to be over-anxious and lacking in self-confidence; but they are also bound to have latent feelings of rebellion and self-assertion. They perhaps want to claim their independence and find their own identity, but are held back by fear of losing security and parental approval. This is certainly true of Winnie, who had her full share of healthy ambition. And being a Victorian daughter, and the virtue of 'home-duties' unquestioned, she experienced the conflict in an acute form.

Attacks of asthma have often been found to have been triggered off by a threat of parting from the beloved parent, which would imply a situation in which the patient is forced into independence. Once the link between fear and asthma is physically established, the patient may of course suffer attacks in different sorts of anxious situations. But basically this does seem to be what happened to Winnie. It is likely that she was ill in 1882 when all her conscious desires were fixed on marriage; she had attacks off and on during the next three years, while she was still struggling to resign herself to Papa's veto; the decision to go to Newnham renewed the conflict – she became quite ill in Switzerland shortly after hearing that she had been accepted. Maybe if she had been left at Newnham to fight it out alone she would have won through, maybe not. As it was, she came home and allowed herself to be made an invalid. And the attack that killed her came shortly after she had begun to make serious plans about starting work again. And yet all her *conscious* self was making passionate plans to escape, to work, to live her own life.

An attack of asthma has the significance of a suppressed cry. It has been found that if patients can be induced to indulge in unrestrained crying, they are often eased and the asthma abated. Similarly the unburdening of the sufferer's anxieties to doctor or confidant has the same releasing effect.

But Winnie aimed at self-control and Christian resignation, and she never complained. The nearest she ever got to crying out and putting into words the conflicts which were, quite literally, choking her, was in her letter to Lina of November 19, which contains the most direct and revealing things she ever said about herself – and yet she apologised for writing it. Lina could perhaps have helped her; but Lina could not know what Winnie so desperately needed, and Winnie was too confused to pursue her self-analysis on her own. With her other great friend Meta, she had got into the way of projecting chiefly her cerebral and 'saintly' side; she did not cry out to Meta.

Inability to swallow or to speak is a not infrequent symptom of extreme tension. The most usual treatment for tension in the past was complete rest with no intellectual stimulus or exciting visitors. For many, as for Winnie, this merely aggravated the symptoms. And this meant that Winnie could eat progressively less and less, so that her physical state was inadequate to stand up to her attacks of asthma; which gave her an increased fear of asthma, which heightened the tension. It was a vicious circle.

The medical treatment that Winnie received was futile by modern standards. Of course modern drugs could have helped her; twentieth-century Winnie need not die. Equally well she in 1885 need not have died, had she been encouraged to talk out her anxieties. Her doctors had always considered her troubles to be 'nervous'; her sisters thought so too, and so did Papa. And so they all did what they thought was best – they did everything they could to keep her quiet. They admired the stoical self-control that she never lost in their presence. If some inspired friend could have broken doctor's orders and Winnie's own inhibitions, perhaps she could have been helped to loosen the deadlock between her desire to go into the world and her fear of it.

Winnie was left stranded on the shores of the nineteenth century. Her portrait, which stood on the drawing-room piano until the Hermitage was dismantled, saw most of the people she loved go forward into the twentieth: some into situations and opportunities that she would have welcomed for them, a few into tragedy.

*

Meta Tuke stayed in academic life. She read Modern Languages at Newnham and got her first in 1888. She was a lecturer at Newnham until 1905, and in 1907 was appointed Principal of Bedford College, a post in which her academic and administrative skills were stretched to their utmost. She made a great Principal. In 1932 she was made a Dame of the British Empire, and in 1939 published her *History of Bedford College*. Meta never married. She always saw a lot of the young Lindsells, her sister Minnie's children, and always had a great many devoted friends, some dating from her Newnham days. Greatly honoured and greatly loved, Dame Margaret Tuke died in 1947.

Mrs Marshall lived until 1944. After her husband's death in 1924 his library was amalgamated with the existing economics collection in the Cambridge University Library to form the Marshall Library, where Mrs Marshall for many years worked as custodian and librarian. There is a photograph of her working in the Marshall Library, white-haired and wearing a tailor-made suit. She learnt to be at home in our world, the world of mass media and instant culture. Did she ever think back to the far-off golden days of Newnham, when she and Jane Harrison sat in the shade embroidering pomegranates and Virginia creeper on their dresses, and chaperoned each other out to tea?

Lina Bronner's doctor father died in January 1886, which interrupted her Newnham life as she went home to her family in Bradford for some weeks. On her return to Cambridge she went over to Hitchin one day with Hugh to meet Winnie's family. She went down from Cambridge the following year without taking her Tripos. In 1891 she married a Dr A. Cahn of Strasbourg, and her married life was spent on the continent. Lina had two children, Carl and Greta, both of whom followed in the family tradition and became doctors. Lina lived through two world wars and lost her home each time. In 1938, now a widow, she was taken by her daughter to safety in Switzerland. Her son Carl went to America. Heartbroken by the separation, Lina died soon afterwards in Basle.

Cousin Ted, Uncle Henry's theatrical son, died in New York in 1888 while still in his twenties in unexplained and somewhat sinister circumstances.

Harley Rodney spent all his working life at the Public Record Office and his spare time working at the Christ Church Mission in Poplar. He was an amateur musician and a chess player of repute. When he retired he bought the Villa Julia at High Wickham, near Hastings, where he lived until his death in 1930. He never married. His obituary in the *Times* referred to him as 'essentially a man's man', and praised his 'sense of proportion, unwearied patience and energy, and ability to take long views'.

Juliet, Esther, Freda and Hilda grew older and no prettier and more and more absorbed by family and local matters. 'The Hermits', as they called themselves, retained the magic of their childhood into middle-age. Any drama that was missing from their lives they could quite well supply for themselves. They gave a New Year Party in the 1890's, for which they all dressed up as monks and processed around the Hermitage, up and down the various flights of stairs, chanting and carrying tapers, with Hugh at the head declaiming *The Jackdaw of Rheims*. 'It was a very *unusual* party' said someone who was there.

The Misses Seebohm and their brother bear a strong resemblance, both in attitude and upbringing, to the Misses Schlegel and their brother in *Howards End* by E. M. Forster, who was himself brought up in Hertfordshire. But there is a radical difference. One of the themes of *Howards End* is the importance for a human being of reconciling the 'monk' and the 'beast' within him; reconciling, that is, his controlled civilized self with his uncontrollable instinctive self. This the Misses Schlegel, for all their high-mindedness, were able to do. The Seebohms, on the other hand, seem to have had sometimes a Cornelian disregard for the passions; especially when they manifested themselves in other members of the family. The 'monk' seems to have had the upper hand. Forster wrote in *Howards End*:

> Only connect! Only connect the prose and the passion, and both will be exalted, and human love will be seen at its height. Live in fragments no longer. Only connect, and the beast and the monk, robbed of the isolation that is life to either, will die'.

In 1891 Juliet, at the age of thirty-two, was married in ivory velvet to Mr Rickman John Godlee. Her husband later became surgeon-in-ordinary to the Royal Family, President of the Royal College of Surgeons, biographer of his uncle, Lord Lister, and was knighted. With him Juliet led a happy, cultivated and comfortable life. But her decision to marry – a most legitimate and unhurried step towards an independent life – was greeted at the Hermitage with despair and cries of alarm. How *brave* Mother was being to allow Juliet to leave home! how *dreadful* for them all to have to do without her!

The cries of alarm were even more desperate when dearest Hugh at the age of thirty-six became engaged to Miss Leslie Gribble, who was young, gay, and not particularly erudite by Seebohm standards. How *would* Papa manage without Hugh? And Miss Gribble, they said (including Lady Godlee, but excluding gentle Freda), did not seem to have much to say for herself. The family professed itself astonished when the engagement was announced, even though Hugh had been in love with Leslie since she had been a school-girl. Leslie had attended the same boarding-school in St Andrews as Hugh's little cousin Mabel Elizabeth; Hugh and Leslie had corresponded via Mabel. This same little Mabel recalled calling at the Hermitage one Sunday morning when Hugh had just broken the news of his engagement to his parents and sisters. All the family were upset and nervous, but nobody volunteered an explanation for the very apparent tension. Mother died immediately after Hugh's marriage, while he and Leslie were abroad on their honeymoon.

Hugh and Leslie had four children and were happy until in 1913 Leslie died with complications in another pregnancy. Hugh continued living with his young family at Poynders End, the house he had built near Hitchin, and there he remained, following in Papa's footsteps. He had joined Sharples Bank as a partner in 1892, and when in 1896 Sharples was absorbed by Barclays (after some disagreement with the Tukes) he became Local Director. Hugh was a successful banker, and became in due course vice-chairman and deputy-chairman of Barclays Bank, and in 1934 was appointed chairman of Barclays (France). But for Hugh as for his father, nothing was more important than local life and local matters. Hugh was Governor of the Grammar School in Hitchin and a member of the Herts Education Committee. He was involved in or consulted on everything that went on in the town. In 1933 he was married again, to Mrs Marjorie Lyall, and he died in 1946.

Freda, like Winnie, was a casualty. From childhood, as her mother had recorded, she had been 'sensitive in mind and body'. She loved children and was devoted to her Friends' Sunday School Class. In 1903 she published *Notes of Sunday Talks with Children*. She, Esther and Hilda were all governers of Hitchin schools; but Freda would have liked to involve herself further and teach professionally. She was dissuaded. Pious and sentimental, she never found a part to play in life. Maybe she also suffered through not having such high-powered intellectual equipment as the rest of the family.

Someone's voice from the past is reported as having said darkly: 'Freda oughtn't to have been born'. At any rate her problems led her into psychosis. As the years passed she suffered recurring bouts of emotional disturbance, after which she would be sent off to recuperate abroad. From there she would write to her sisters begging them to talk to her about her trouble when she came home, as their silence was the worst thing to bear. But on her return they never mentioned what had happened.

Finally Freda went away for good. (Another unidentified voice from the past: 'She turned violent on Esther.') She went into an institution, where she died in 1936. Hugh's children – Derrick, Frederic, George and Fidelity – knew nothing of the existence of their aunt Freda until they were grown up.

Now only Esther and Hilda were left at home. After the desolation of Papa's death in 1912 they stayed on at the Hermitage until it was sold up after the first war. The breaking-up of the family home was a formidable task. The Seebohms were hoarders, they had kept everything. The attics were full of their old toys which had rarely been brought out for visiting children. Downstairs there were piles of notes, papers, books, articles, offprints, periodicals, music, letters, drawings, invitations and catalogues, stuffed in every cupboard, piled on every surface and lying in stacks behind sofas and armchairs. Esther went through everything, and spent days and months filing, labelling, selectively preserving and destroying. Papa's economics books went to the Maitland Library in Oxford, other valuable works to the Bodleian and to the British Museum.

Then Esther and Hilda moved to Fairfield, the old Ransom house where Winnie had died, and rechristened it Little Benslow Hills.

They were no longer young, but they were wealthy and cultured. Since the nineties all the Seebohm daughters had travelled widely and enterprisingly. They had been to Egypt and Palestine and Hilda had gone round the world. Now Hilda began to enjoy ill-health – she had been famous as a girl for collapsing on to the sofa the moment Mother temporarily vacated it. Esther, the family curator, looked after Hilda too. It is said that Hilda used to refer facetiously to an admirer of Esther's 'who so thoughtfully *died*' – otherwise Esther might not have been around to minister to her in her illnesses. Hilda had the reputation of being outspoken and critical. She had alienated Aunt Maria, Uncle Henry's widow, by saying sharply when after long years she remarried: 'You shouldn't have done that'.

Hilda died in 1931. Esther lived on for another twenty years, reticent and serene and much loved. She was ninety years old when she died in 1951. Her friends used to say that as she got older she came to resemble more and more the portraits of Erasmus that hung about the house.

*

The Hermits were good people. All their lives they tried to do good, all their lives they loved their neighbours. Better than their neighbours they loved Papa and each other. For some of them the family embrace became a stranglehold; for all of them perhaps it was a little constricting.

Some large families have a self-sufficiency and a sort of holy complacency that is to an outsider both irritating and enviable. Such a family can seem totally self-contained and secure, like a walled city. The Seebohms were like that. That was their strength and their weakness.

Choose to remember them with love. Imagine them far away, as on a flickering film, as Winnie described them one Sunday afternoon before they all had to grow up:

Mother and the girls, in summer dresses, are having tea under the acacia tree in the Hermitage garden. A familiar voice is heard: 'Hello! is there a cup of tea for *me?*' It is Hugh, home unexpectedly from Rugby. Esther and little Hilda run in jubilation to the Bank to tell Papa that Hugh is come. Papa comes home early to enjoy him. Winnie runs over to the shop to buy new tennis balls for a celebration game. Juliet orders fresh tea. The family is together. Leave them together, leave them alone.

But they are all dead now.

Select Bibliography

ANNAN, N., *Leslie Stephen*, Macgibbon & Kee, 1951.

BIRRELL, A., *Frederick Locker-Lampson – a Character Sketch*, Constable, 1920.

BOBBITT, M. R., *With Dearest Love to All: The life and letters of Lady Jebb*, Faber & Faber, 1960.

BRITTAIN, V., *Women at Oxford*, Harrap, 1960.

CLOUGH, B. A., *A Memoir of Anne Jemima Clough*, Edward Arnold, 1897.

DUNBAR, F., *Mind and Body: Psychosomatic Medicine*, New York, Random House, 1955.

FISHER, H. A. L., 'Paul Vinogradoff – a Memoir' in *The Collected Papers of Paul Vinogradoff*, Clarendon Press, 1928, pp. 1–74.

HAMILTON, M. A., *Newnham – an informal biography*, Faber & Faber, 1936.

HINE, R.L., *Hitchin Worthies*, Allen & Unwin, 1932.

LOCKER-LAMPSON, F., *My Confidences* (ed. A. Birrell), Smith, Elder, 1896.

LYND, H. M., *England in the Eighteen-eighties*, O.U.P., 1945.

MARSHALL, M. P., *What I remember*, C.U.P., 1947.

MULLER, M., *Life and letters of Max Müller* (ed. by his wife), Longmans, Green & Co., 1902.

NEWMAN, C., *The Evolution of Medical Education in the Nineteenth Century*, O.U.P., 1957.

NIGHTINGALE, F., 'Cassandra' in *The Cause* by Ray Strachey, G. Bell & Sons, 1928, pp. 395–418.

RYE, W., *A History of Norfolk*, Elliott Stock, 1895.

[SIDGWICK] A. S. & E. M. S., *Henry Sidgwick – a Memoir*, Macmillan, 1906.

TUKE, M. J., *History of Bedford College*, O.U.P., 1939.

VANSITTART, J. (ed.), *Katharine Fry's Book*, Hodder & Stoughton, 1966.

VINOGRADOFF, P., 'Obituary – Frederic Seebohm' in *The Collected Papers of Paul Vinogradoff*, Clarendon Press, 1928, pp. 272–76.

Index

117

VIRAGO MODERN CLASSICS
&
CLASSIC NON-FICTION

The first Virago Modern Classic, *Frost in May* by Antonia White, was published in 1978. It launched a list dedicated to the celebration of women writers and to the rediscovery and reprinting of their works. Its aim was, and is, to demonstrate the existence of a female tradition in fiction, and to broaden the sometimes narrow definition of a 'classic' which has often led to the neglect of interesting novels and short stories. Published with new introductions by some of today's best writers, the books are chosen for many reasons: they may be great works of fiction; they may be wonderful period pieces; they may reveal particular aspects of women's lives; they may be classics of comedy or storytelling.

The companion series, Virago Classic Non-Fiction, includes diaries, letters, literary criticism, and biographies – often by and about authors published in the Virago Modern Classics series.

'Good news for everyone writing and reading today' – *Hilary Mantel*

'A continuingly magnificent imprint' – *Joanna Trollope*

'The Virago Modern Classics have reshaped literary history and enriched the reading of us all. No library is complete without them' – *Margaret Drabble*

VIRAGO MODERN CLASSICS
&
CLASSIC NON-FICTION

Some of the authors included in these two series –

Elizabeth von Arnim, Dorothy Baker, Pat Barker, Nina Bawden,
Nicola Beauman, Sybille Bedford, Jane Bowles, Kay Boyle,
Vera Brittain, Leonora Carrington, Angela Carter, Willa Cather,
Colette, Ivy Compton-Burnett, E.M. Delafield, Maureen Duffy,
Elaine Dundy, Nell Dunn, Emily Eden, George Egerton,
George Eliot, Miles Franklin, Mrs Gaskell,
Charlotte Perkins Gilman, George Gissing,
Victoria Glendinning, Radclyffe Hall, Shirley Hazzard,
Dorothy Hewett, Mary Hocking, Alice Hoffman,
Winifred Holtby, Janette Turner Hospital, Zora Neale Hurston,
Elizabeth Jenkins, F. Tennyson Jesse, Molly Keane,
Margaret Laurence, Maura Laverty, Rosamond Lehmann,
Rose Macaulay, Shena Mackay, Olivia Manning, Paule Marshall,
F.M. Mayor, Anaïs Nin, Kate O'Brien, Olivia, Grace Paley,
Mollie Panter-Downes, Dawn Powell, Dorothy Richardson,
E. Arnot Robertson, Jacqueline Rose, Vita Sackville-West,
Elaine Showalter, May Sinclair, Agnes Smedley, Dodie Smith,
Stevie Smith, Nancy Spain, Christina Stead, Carolyn Steedman,
Gertrude Stein, Jan Struther, Han Suyin, Elizabeth Taylor,
Sylvia Townsend Warner, Mary Webb, Eudora Welty,
Mae West, Rebecca West, Edith Wharton, Antonia White,
Christa Wolf, Virginia Woolf, E.H. Young.

Other Virago Books of Interest

❦

THE TRANSIT OF VENUS

SHIRLEY HAZZARD

Caro, gallant and adventurous, is one of two Australian sisters who have come to post-war England to seek their fortune. Courted long and hopelessly by young scientist, Ted Tice, she is to find that love brings passion, sorrow, betrayal and finally hope. The milder Grace seeks fulfilment in an apparently happy marriage. But, as the decades pass and the characters weave in and out of each other's lives, love, death and two slow-burning secrets wait in ambush for them. Shirley Hazzard, born in Australia, is remarkable for the cosmopolitan range of her fiction 'that lifts the spirit and moves the heart'.

Winner of the USA Book Critics' Circle Award for Best Novel 1980

THE LAND OF SPICES

KATE O'BRIEN

Introduced by Mary Flanagan

'Kate O'Brien's gifts are rich as well as high . . . she has humour at her command as well as poetry' – *Observer*

At a convent in Ireland at the start of the century, Reverend Mother hears little Anna Murphy recite a poem and feels 'a storm break in her hollow heart'. In this beautiful, thoughtful novel Kate O'Brien explores love, forgiveness, freedom and the nature of religious vocation through the stories of both characters. As the Reverend Mother she deals with recalcitrant charges and covertly observes Anna's tribulations while growing up, she learns at last to accept understanding and forgiveness. Kate O'Brien's opposing qualities of faith and luminous intelligence lend this novel a serene poise and passion.

THE DIARIES OF SYLVIA TOWNSEND WARNER

Introduced and edited by Claire Harman

'[Her] heartfelt and heartbroken Diaries give the condensed account of a life at once unassuming and passionate in its devotions – to people and to writing'
– **Andrew Motion**

For Sylvia Townsend Warner the diaries she kept from 1927 to her death in 1978 became the equivalent of an intimate correspondent to whom she could describe and ponder the details of her life. From her thoughts on love, friendship, writing and death to the antics of her cats and plans for her garden, she gives us a self-portrait replete with anecdotes and rich observation. Above all her diaries are a poignant account of her great love affair with Valentine Ackland, a relationship that brought both emotional anguish and sensual liberation.

A VERY GREAT PROFESSION

The Woman's Novel 1914–1939

NICOLA BEAUMAN

'Excellent . . . a loving, historical, sociological portrait'
– **A. S. Byatt**

'Infinitely sharp, subtle and entertaining' – **Molly Keane**

'Katharine was the member of a very great profession which has, as yet, no title and very little recognition . . . She lived at home' – Virginia Woolf, *Night and Day*. Drawing on novelists such as May Sinclair, Elinor Glyn, Rebecca West, E.M. Delafield and Rosamund Lehmann, the author gives us new perspectives on women's lives between the wars – romantic love, domestic life and war – as recorded in the fiction of the time.

Books by post

Virago Books are available through mail order or from your local bookshop. Other books which might be of interest include:~

☐ A Very Great Profession	Nicola Beauman	£6.99
☐ Transit of Venus	Shirley Hazzard	£6.99
☐ The Land of Spices	Kate O'Brien	£6.99
☐ The Diaries of Sylvia Townsend Warner	Claire Harman (ed.)	£12.99

Please send Cheque/Eurocheque/Postal Order (sterling only), Access, Visa or Mastercard:

☐☐☐☐☐☐☐☐☐☐☐☐☐☐☐☐

Expiry Date: _____   *Signature:* _____

Please allow 75 pence per book for post and packing in U.K.
Overseas customers please allow £1.00 per copy for post and packing.

All orders to:
Virago Press, Book Service by Post, P.O. Box 29, Douglas,
Isle of Man, IM99 1BQ.   Tel: 01624 675137.   Fax: 01624 670923.

Name: _____

Address: _____

_____

Please allow 20 days for delivery.
Please tick box if you would like to receive a free stock list ☐
Please tick box if you do not wish to receive any additional information ☐

Prices and availability subject to change without notice.